True Blue Lines
God's Laws for Law Enforcement Officers

Curtis Mosley

Photo courtesy of Walton County Sheriff Michael Adkinson

Copyright © 2016 by Curtis Mosley

All rights reserved. No part of this book may be reproduced in any manner without written permission except in the case of brief quotations included in critical articles and reviews. For information, please contact the author.

ISBN: 978-0-692-79801-0

First Edition First Printing

Dedication

I dedicate this book to the fine Law Enforcement Officers throughout the world who have given their lives in the line of duty.

Greater love has no man than this, that a man lay down his life for his friends. - John 15:13

Photo courtesy of Walton County Sheriff Michael Adkinson

Acknowledgments

I would like to express my appreciation to the following professionals who contributed their time and resources to the production of this book:

- Becki Johnston of Radiotronics, Inc. and AceK9.com of Stuart, Florida

- Lani Suchcicki, Copyright Manager, Pensacola News Journal

- Michael A. Adkinson, Sheriff, Walton County, Florida

- Pam Schmidt of PS Graphics of Fredericksburg, Texas

- Paul Lee, Executive Director, Fellowship of Christian Police Officers - USA

- Stephen Carlisle, Police Chief, of the Roman Forest Police Department

- Steve Groeninger, Senior Director of Communications & Marketing at the National Law Enforcement Officers Memorial Fund

Table of Contents

TOPICS

Ability	1
Accountability	3
Active Shooter Situations	4
Attention to Detail	6
Attitude	7
Awards	9
Bravery	10
Change	13
Character	15
Community Involvement	16
Composure	18
Confidence	20
Confidentiality	22
Criminal Minds	23
Danger	25
Deadly Force	28
Decisions	29
Delegation	30
Demonstrations	31
Emergencies	32
Energy and Industry	35
Family	37
Financial Management	38
Friends	41
Grieving	42
Growth and Development	45
Hand to Hand Combat	46
Honesty	47
Humor	49
Image	50
Interpersonal Skills	51
Interrogation	53
Justice	55
Leadership	57
Partners	59
Patrolling	60

Table of Contents continued

Planning 63
Police Dogs 64
Post Traumatic Stress Disorder (PTSD) 65
Prayer 67
Preparation 68
Preventing Suicide 69
Promotion to Higher Responsibility 71
Protecting the Weak 72
Protection 75
Provision 79
Recognizing Elder Abuse 81
Recovering Stolen Property 83
Recruiting 84
Reliability 85
Remembering Crime Victims 87
Reporting 89
Reputation 90
Rest 91
Sergeants, Lieutenants, and Captains 92
Set the Example 95
Special Weapons and Tactics (SWAT) 97
Supervision 99
Teamwork 101
Temptation 103
Terrorism 105
Testifying 107
Tough Times 109
Traffic Control 111
Training 112
Work 114
Working Without Recognition 117

HEROES
Officer John Poulos 120
Officer Timothy Purdy 122
Patrolman Steve Wilson 124
Sergeant Adam Johnson 126

Table of Contents continued

Sergeant Jay Cook 128
Chief of Police Jeffery Walters 130
Officer Jessica Hawkins 132
Corporal James L. Cosby Jr. 134
Sergeant Anthony Schnacky and Officer Matthew Curry ... 136
Officer James Cunningham 138
Sergeant Philip B. Gingerella, Sr. 140
Trooper First Class Joshua Kim 142
Officer Nicholas Simons 144
Deputy U. S. Marshals (DUSMs) Matthew Barger,
   Michael Cifu, Andrew Kottke, and Frank Morales 146
Chief of Police Thomas Fowler, Sergeant Robert Roy,
   Officer Michael Alder, and Officer Justin Murphy 148
Officer Christopher Nebbeling 150
Lieutenant Jerald Wheeler 152
Trooper Brian Beuning 154
Senior Investigator John Vescio 156
Deputy Brian Matthews 158
Officer Matthew Bowling and Officer Vincent Martucci 160
Lieutenant Timothy Jungel 162
Deputy Sheriff Jeffrey Brunkow 164
Officer Sean O'Brien 166
Trooper Rick Carlson, Trooper Jim Leonard,
   Deputy Justin Holzschu 168
Sergeant John Conneely and Officer Michael Modzelewski .. 170
Officer Brenton Medeiros 172
Officer Charles Law 174
Sergeant Nathan Hutchinson 176
Police Officer Randall Courson 178
Customs and Border Patrol Agent Travis Creteau 180
Officers Rade Momirovich and Covelle Padgett 182
Trooper Jaime Ablett, Officer Daniel Krause
   and Officer Laura Winkel 184
Border Patrol Agent Jared A. Monnett 186
Watertown (Massachusetts) Police Officers 188
Deputy Sheriff Elton R. Simmons 192

Photo courtesy of Walton County Sheriff Michael Adkinson

ABILITY

The Lord put you in this profession. You are able. Step up.

And the LORD looked upon him, and said, Go in this your might, and you shall save Israel ... have not I sent you? (Judges 6:14)

I will praise thee; for I am fearfully and wonderfully made: Marvelous are your works; And that my soul knows right well. (Psalm 139:14)

God created man in his own image. (Genesis 1:27)

I can do all things through Christ which strengthens me. (Philippians 4:13)

With God's help, things are going to work out much better than you expect.

Let us go up at once, and possess it; for we are well able to overcome it. (Numbers 13:30)

For by you I have run through a troop; And by my God have I leaped over a wall. (Psalm 18:29)

Arise, for it is your task, and we are with you; be strong and do it." (Ezra 10:4)

"I can do nothing on my own. As I hear, I judge, and my judgment is just, because I seek not my own will but the will of him who sent me. (John 5:30)

ABILITY

I am the vine; you are the branches. Whoever abides in me and I in him, he it is that bears much fruit, for apart from me you can do nothing. (John 15:5)

Now unto him that is able to do exceeding abundantly above all that we ask or think, according to the power that works in us. (Ephesians 3:20)

Are you called to help others? Do it with all the strength and energy that God supplies. (1 Peter 4:11, TLB)

As each has received a gift, use it to serve one another, as good stewards of God's varied grace. (1 Peter 4:10)

ACCOUNTABILITY

Make sure you are proud of the person in the mirror.

Each of us will give an account of himself to God. (Romans 14:12)

Then the disciples, every man according to his ability, determined to send relief unto the brethren which dwelt in Judaea: which also they did, and sent it to the elders by the hands of Barnabas and Saul. (Acts 11:28-30)

Let the righteous smite me; it shall be a kindness: and let him reprove me; it shall be an excellent oil. (Psalm 141:5)

Open rebuke is better than secret love. Faithful are the wounds of a friend. (Proverbs 27:5, 6)

For unto whomsoever much is given, of him shall be much required: and to whom men have committed much, of him they will ask the more. (Luke 12:48)

You have been trusted with substantial authority. Use it to serve the community.

But I say unto you, That every idle word that men shall speak, they shall give account thereof in the day of judgment. (Matthew 12:36)

Photo courtesy of Walton County Sheriff Michael Adkinson

ACTIVE SHOOTER SITUATIONS

It's O.K. to ask God to help. Do your best and leave the rest to Him. You can't have a testimony without a test.

Beloved, think it not strange concerning the fiery trial which is to try you, as though some strange thing happened unto you. (1 Peter 4:12)

Behold, the wicked bend the bow; they have fitted their arrow to the string to shoot in the dark at the upright in heart. (Psalm 11:2, ESV)

Use offensive tactics.

Fight as never before. (1 Samuel 4:9, NLT)

For by you I have run through a troop; and by my God have I leaped over a wall. (Psalm 18:29)

Your hand will find out all your enemies; your right hand will find out those who hate you. You will make them as a blazing oven when you appear. The LORD will swallow them up in his wrath, and fire will consume them. (Psalms 21:8-9)

And though they hide themselves in the top of Carmel, I will search and take them out thence. (Amos 9:3)

ACTIVE SHOOTER SITUATIONS

Protect yourself.

Put on the whole armor. (Ephesians 6:11, ESV)

Arise, O LORD, disappoint him, cast him down: Deliver my soul from the wicked. (Psalm 17:13)

For in the time of trouble he shall hide me. (Psalm 27:5)

For he shall give his angels charge over you, to keep thee in all your ways. (Psalm 91:11)

Our soul is escaped as a bird out of the snare of the fowlers: The snare is broken, and we are escaped. Our help is in the name of the LORD. (Psalm 124:7–8)

Keep me from the snares which they have laid for me. (Psalm 141:9)

The LORD is your security. He will keep your foot from being caught in a trap. (Proverbs 3:26)

ATTENTION TO DETAIL

❧

Most operations run, but not many hum.

The little foxes are ruining the vineyards. (Song of Solomon 2:15, TLB)

According to all that I show you, after the pattern of the tabernacle, and the pattern of all the instruments thereof, even so shall you make it. (Exodus 25:9)

"All this," David said, "I have in writing as a result of the LORD's hand on me, and he enabled me to understand all the details of the plan." (1 Chronicles 28:19)

And see if there be any wicked way in me. (Psalm 139:24)

See, says he, that you make all things according to the pattern showed to you in the mount. (Hebrews 8:5)

Let us lay aside every weight, and the sin which does so easily beset us, and let us run with patience the race that is set before us. (Hebrews 12:1)

ATTITUDE

If you're happy, show it. Make someone's day.

At last the wall was completed to half its height around the entire city, for the people had worked with enthusiasm. (Nehemiah 4:6, TLB)

When a man is gloomy, everything seems to go wrong; when he is cheerful, everything seems right! (Proverbs 15:15, TLB)

Do all things without murmurings and disputings: That you may be blameless and harmless, the sons of God, without rebuke, in the midst of a crooked and perverse nation, among whom you shine as lights in the world. (Philippians 2:14)

A joyful heart is good medicine, but a crushed spirit dries up the bones. (Proverbs 17:22, ESV)

Used with permission by John and Becki Johnston from AceK9.com.
Manufacturing life saving equipment for 30 years, honoring our heroes by capturing memorable moments.

AWARDS

AWARDS

Recognition motivates.

Do you know a hard-working man? He shall be successful and stand before kings. (Proverbs 22:29, TLB)

David asked the men standing near him, "What will be done for the man who kills this Philistine and removes this disgrace from Israel? (1 Samuel 17:26, NIV)

Humble yourselves in the sight of the Lord, and he shall lift you up. (James 4:10)

Render therefore to all their dues: tribute to whom tribute is due... honor to whom honor. (Romans 13:7)

Men will praise you, when you do well for yourself. (Psalm 49:18)

I considered all travail, and every right work, that for this a man is envied of his neighbor. (Ecclesiastes 4:4)

The glory of children are their fathers. (Proverbs 17:6)

Like one who binds the stone in the sling is one who gives honor to a fool. (Proverbs 26:8, ESV)

Follow the Lord's rules for doing his work, just as an athlete either follows the rules or is disqualified and wins no prize. (2 Timothy 2:5, TLB)

For the Lord's sake, submit to all human authority—whether the king as head of state, or the officials he has appointed. For the king has sent them to punish those who do wrong and to honor those who do right. (1 Peter 2:13-14, NLT)

BRAVERY

Bravery is good. Recklessness is bad.

Have I not commanded you? Be strong and courageous. Do not be frightened, and do not be dismayed, for the LORD your God is with you wherever you go." (Joshua 1:9)

Be strong and courageous. Do not fear or be in dread of them, for it is the LORD your God who goes with you. He will not leave you or forsake you." (Deuteronomy 31:6)

For God alone, O my soul, wait in silence, for my hope is from him. He only is my rock and my salvation, my fortress; I shall not be shaken. (Psalm 62:5)

The path of the godly leads to life. So why fear death? (Proverbs 12:28)

If God is for us, who can be against us? (Romans 8:31)

You are from God and have overcome them, for he who is in you is greater than he who is in the world. (1 John 4:4)

I can do all things through him who strengthens me. (Philippians 4:13)

Be watchful, stand firm in the faith, act like men, be strong. (1 Corinthians 16:13)

On the day I called, you answered me; my strength of soul you increased. (Psalm 138:3)

BRAVERY

David strengthened himself in the Lord. He remembered that God was bigger than any enemy he faced.

A man's courage can sustain his broken body, but when courage dies, what hope is left? (Proverbs 18:14, TLB)

The wicked flee when no one is chasing them! But the godly are bold as lions! (Proverbs 28:1, TLB)

But the Lord God says, ... If you want me to protect you, you must learn to believe what I say. (Isaiah 8:7,9)

Don't fear anything except the Lord of the armies of heaven! If you fear him, you need fear nothing else. He will be your safety. (Isaiah 8:13-14)

For God has not given us the spirit of fear; but of power, and of love, and of a sound mind. (2 Timothy 1:7)

The Lord is my helper, and I will not fear what man shall do unto me. (Hebrews 13:6)

CHANGE

Photo courtesy of Walton County Sheriff Michael Adkinson

CHANGE

The river is always moving, but if you're standing on the Rock, you won't get swept away.

Any enterprise is built by wise planning, becomes strong through common sense, and profits wonderfully by keeping abreast of the facts. (Proverbs 24:3-4, TLB)

Do not be anxious about anything, but in everything by prayer and supplication with thanksgiving let your requests be made known to God. And the peace of God, which surpasses all understanding, will guard your hearts and your minds in Christ Jesus.
(Philippians 4:6-7)

Jesus Christ the same yesterday, and to day, and for ever.
(Hebrews 13:8)

There is a right time for everything:... A time for keeping; A time for throwing away. (Ecclesiastes 3:1, 6, TLB)

Behold, I will do a new thing; Now it shall spring forth; shall you not know it?

I will even make a way in the wilderness, And rivers in the desert.
(Isaiah 43:19)

CHARACTER

Used with permission by John and Becki Johnston from AceK9.com.
Manufacturing life saving equipment for 30 years, honoring our heroes by capturing memorable moments.

CHARACTER

Nothing is more fun than a clean life.

A man is known by his actions. An evil man lives an evil life; a good man lives a godly life. (Proverbs 21:8, TLB)

A man who loves pleasure becomes poor; wine and luxury are not the way to riches! (Proverbs 18:5, TLB)

A good man loves justice, but it is a calamity to evil-doers. (Proverbs 21:15, TLB)

The man who tries to be good, loving and kind finds life, righteousness and honor. (Proverbs 21:21, TLB)

Dead men don't sin:

I am crucified with Christ: nevertheless I live; yet not I, but Christ lives in me: and the life which I now live in the flesh I live by the faith of the Son of God, who loved me, and gave himself for me. (Galatians 2:20)

Likewise reckon (believe it to be true) you also yourselves to be dead indeed unto sin, but alive unto God through Jesus Christ our Lord. Let not sin therefore reign in your mortal body, that you should obey it in the lusts thereof. Neither yield you your members as instruments of unrighteousness unto sin: but yield yourselves unto God, as those that are alive from the dead, and your members as instruments of righteousness unto God. (Romans 6:11-13)

COMMUNITY INVOLVEMENT

You are a vital contributor to the community.

And work for the peace and prosperity of the city where I sent you ... Pray to the LORD for it, for its welfare will determine your welfare. (Jeremiah 29:7)

First of all, then, I urge that petitions, prayers, intercessions, and thanksgiving be offered on behalf of all men for kings and all those in authority, so that we may lead tranquil and quiet lives in all godliness and dignity. (2 Timothy 2:1-2, Berean Study Bible)

Everyone must submit himself to the governing authorities, for there is no authority except that which is from God. The authorities that exist have been appointed by God. Consequently, the one who resists authority is opposing what God has set in place, and those who do so will bring judgment on themselves. (Romans 13:1-2)

On their arrival in Capernaum, the collectors of the Temple tax came to Peter and asked him, "Doesn't your teacher pay the Temple tax?" "Yes, he does." (Matthew 17:24-25, NLT)

And if you draw out your soul to the hungry, and satisfy the afflicted soul; then shall your light rise in obscurity, and your darkness be as the noonday. (Isaiah 58:10)

Blessed are they who observe justice, who do righteousness at all times! (Psalm 106:3-4, ESV)

You shall love your neighbor as yourself. (Mark 12:31)

COMMUNITY INVOLVEMENT

Photo courtesy of Chief Stephen Carlisle, Roman Forest Police Department

COMPOSURE

Things don't happen to us: they happen for us. Keep your eye on the prize.

A short-tempered man is a fool. He hates the man who is patient. (Proverbs 14:17, TLB)

A soft answer turns away wrath, but a harsh word stirs up anger. (Proverbs 15:1)

It is better to be slow-tempered than famous; it is better to have self-control than to control an army. (Proverbs 16:32).

Peace I leave with you; my peace I give to you. Not as the world gives do I give to you. Let not your hearts be troubled, neither let them be afraid, (John 14:27)

Even though I walk through the valley of the shadow of death, I will fear no evil, for you are with me. (Psalm 23:4)

Casting all your care upon him; for he cares for you. (1 Peter 5:7)

But whoever listens to me will dwell secure and will be at ease, without dread of disaster. (Proverbs 1:33)

The vexation of a fool is known at once, but the prudent ignores an insult. (Proverbs 12:16, ESV)

Whoever is slow to anger has great understanding. (Proverbs 14:29, ESV)

He that has no rule over his own spirit is like a city that is broken down, and without walls. (Proverbs 25:28)

COMPOSURE

Fear not, stand still, and see the salvation of the LORD, which he will show to you today. (Exodus 14:13)

You will keep him in perfect peace, whose mind is stayed on you: because he trusts in you. (Isaiah 26:3)

The earnest prayer of a righteous person has great power and produces wonderful results. (James 5:16, NLT)

CONFIDENCE

❧

Leave the outcome to God.

Tackle every task that comes along, and if you fear God you can expect his blessing. (Ecclesiastes 7:18, TLB)

I am fearfully and wonderfully made: marvelous are your works; and that my soul knows right well. (Psalm 139:14)

For the LORD shall be your confidence, And shall keep your foot from being taken. (Proverbs 3:26)

Fear you not; for I am with you: Be not dismayed; for I am your God: I will strengthen you; yes, I will help you; Yes, I will uphold you with the right hand of my righteousness. (Isaiah 41:10)

Not that we are sufficient of ourselves to think any thing as of ourselves; but our sufficiency is of God. (2 Corinthians 3:5-6).

Stand. (Ephesians 6:13)

Go in this your might. (Judges 6:14)

Be strong! Be courageous! Do not be afraid of them! For the Lord your God will be with you. He will neither fail you nor forsake you. (Deuteronomy 31:6)

Being confident of this very thing, that he which has begun a good work in you will perform it until the day of Jesus Christ. (Philippians 1:6)

If God is for us, who can be against us? (Romans 8:31)

CONFIDENCE

There is no reason to be intimidated.

Men are nothing but a mere breath; human beings are unreliable. When they are weighed in the scales, all of them together are lighter than air. (Psalm 62:9)

Photo courtesy of Walton County Sheriff Michael Adkinson

CONFIDENTIALITY

You must be trustworthy with information.

A gossip goes around spreading rumors, while a trustworthy man tries to quiet them. (Proverbs 11:13, TLB)

Don't be hot-headed and rush to court! You may start something you can't finish and go down before your neighbor in shameful defeat. So discuss the matter with him privately. Don't tell anyone else, lest he accuse you of slander and you can't withdraw what you said. (Proverbs 25:8-10, TLB)

He that covers a transgression seeks love; But he that repeats a matter separates very friends. (Proverbs 17:9)

CRIMINAL MINDS

When drugs enter, logic leaves.

An evil man's mind is crammed with lies. (Proverbs 12:5)

An evil man loves to harm others; being a good neighbor is out of his line. (Proverbs 21:10)

The wicked enjoy fellowship with others who are wicked; liars enjoy liars. (Proverbs 17:4)

Evil men don't understand the importance of justice, but those who follow the Lord are much concerned about it. (Proverbs 28:5, TLB)

They have plotted to call for a mob to lynch you. Don't trust them, no matter how pleasantly they speak. Don't believe them. (Jeremiah 12:6, TLB)

The heart is deceitful above all things, and desperately sick; who can understand it? (Jeremiah 17:9)

Can...a leopard take away his spots? Nor can you who are so used to doing evil now start being good. (Jeremiah 13:23, TLB).

The thief comes only to steal and kill and destroy. (John 10:10)

The good hate the badness of the wicked. The wicked hate the goodness of the good. (Proverbs 29:27, TLB)

Because God does not punish sinners instantly, people feel it is safe to do wrong. (Ecclesiastes 8:11, TLB)

One fate comes to all. That is why men are not more careful to be good, but instead choose their own mad course, for they have no hope – there is nothing but death ahead anyway. (Ecclesiastes 9:3, TLB)

DANGER

Photo courtesy of Walton County Sheriff Michael Adkinson

DANGER

❧

When there's smoke in the air and the flames are flashing around your feet, Jesus will show up. "I see four men, unbound, walking around in the fire unharmed! And the fourth looks like a god!" (Daniel 3:25)

A wise man is cautious and avoids danger; a fool plunges ahead with great confidence. (Proverbs 14:16, TLB)

You even keep me from getting into trouble! (Psalm 32:7, TLB)

A prudent man foresees the difficulties ahead and prepares for them; the simpleton goes blindly on and suffers the consequences. (Proverbs 22:3)

Only a simpleton believes what he is told! A prudent man checks to see where he is going. (Proverbs 14:15, TLB)

It is safer to meet a bear robbed of her cubs than to confront a fool caught in foolishness. (Proverbs 17:12)

Desire without knowledge is not good, and whoever makes haste with his feet misses his way. (Proverbs 19:2)

Two are better than one; because they have a good reward for their labor. For if they fall, the one will lift up his fellow: but woe to him that is alone when he falls; for he has not another to help him up. (Ecclesiastes 4:9-10)

When you lie down, you shall not be afraid: Yes, you shall lie down, and your sleep shall be sweet. (Proverbs 3:24)

Fear you not; for I am with you: Be not dismayed; for I am your God: I will strengthen you; yes, I will help you; Yes, I will uphold you with the right hand of my righteousness. (Isaiah 41:10)

But even the very hairs of your head are all numbered. Fear not therefore. (Luke 12:7)

DANGER

When you pass through the waters, I will be with you; and through the rivers, they shall not overflow you. When you walk through the fire, you shall not be burned, nor shall the flame scorch you. (Isaiah 43:2, NKJV)

Psalm 91
He that dwells in the secret place of the most High
Shall abide under the shadow of the Almighty.
I will say of the LORD, He is my refuge and my fortress:
My God; in him will I trust.
Surely he shall deliver you from the snare of the fowler,
And from the noisome pestilence.
He shall cover you with his feathers,
And under his wings shall you trust:
His truth shall be your shield and buckler.
Your shall not be afraid for the terror by night;
Nor for the arrow that flies by day;
Nor for the pestilence that walks in darkness;
Nor for the destruction that wastes at noonday.
A thousand shall fall at thy side,
And ten thousand at thy right hand;
But it shall not come nigh you.
Only with thine eyes shall you behold
And see the reward of the wicked.
Because you have made the LORD, which is my refuge,
Even the most High, your habitation;
There shall no evil befall you,
Neither shall any plague come nigh your dwelling.
For he shall give his angels charge over you,
To keep you in all your ways.
They shall bear your up in their hands,
Lest you dash your foot against a stone.
You shall tread upon the lion and adder:
The young lion and the dragon shall you trample under feet.
Because he has set his love upon me, therefore will I deliver him:
I will set him on high, because he has known my name.
He shall call upon me, and I will answer him:
I will be with him in trouble;
I will deliver him, and honor him.
With long life will I satisfy him,
And show him my salvation.

DEADLY FORCE

Photo courtesy of Walton County Sheriff Michael Adkinson

DEADLY FORCE

Whosoever hates his brother is a murderer: and you know that no murderer has eternal life abiding in him. (1 John 3:15)

But evil words come from an evil heart and defile the man who says them. For from the heart come evil thoughts, murder, adultery, fornication, theft, lying, and slander. (Matthew 15:18-19)

If a thief is caught in the act of breaking into a house and is killed, the one who killed him is not guilty. (Exodus 22:2, TLB).

But understand this: If the owner of the house had known at what time of night the thief was coming, he would have kept watch and would not have let his house be broken into. (Matthew 24:43)

A man can prevent trouble from thieves by keeping watch for them. (Matthew 24:43, TLB)

He does not bear the sword in vain. For he is the servant of God, an avenger who carries out God's wrath on the wrongdoer. (Romans 13:4, ESV)

Whoever sheds the blood of man, by man shall his blood be shed, for God made man in his own image. (Genesis 9:6)

The king allowed the Jews who were in every city to gather and defend their lives, to destroy, to kill, and to annihilate any armed force of any people or province that might attack them, children and women included, and to plunder their goods. (Esther, 8:11, ESV)

For everything there is a season, and a time for every matter under heaven…a time to kill. (Ecclesiastes 3:1,3, ESV)

I stationed the people by their clans, with their swords, their spears, and their bows. And I looked and arose and said to the nobles and to the officials and to the rest of the people, "Do not be afraid of them. Remember the Lord, who is great and awesome, and fight for your brothers, your sons, your daughters, your wives, and your homes." (Nehemiah 4:13-14, ESV)

DECISIONS

Follow your logic out before you decide. What will happen if each course of action is taken?

In all your ways acknowledge him, and he will make straight your paths. (Proverbs 3:6)

I will instruct you and teach you in the way you should go; I will counsel you with my eye upon you. (Psalm 32:8)

Nevertheless, I am continually with you; you hold my right hand. You guide me with your counsel. (Psalm 73:23)

DELEGATION

Delegation is the secret to management; if it's done right.

Entrust to reliable people. (2 Timothy 2:2, NIV)

Putting confidence in an unreliable person in times of trouble is like chewing with a broken tooth or walking on a lame foot. (Proverbs 25:19, NLT)

"Find some capable, godly, honest men who hate bribes, and appoint them as judges, one judge for each 1000 people; he in turn will have ten judges under him, each in charge of a hundred; and under each of them will be two judges, each responsible for the affairs of fifty people; and each of these will have five judges beneath him, each counseling ten persons. 22 Let these men be responsible to serve the people with justice at all times. Anything that is too important or complicated can be brought to you. But the smaller matters they can take care of themselves. That way it will be easier for you because you will share the burden with them. (Exodus 18:21-23, TLB)

Photo courtesy of Chief Stephen Carlisle, Roman Forest Police Department

DEMONSTRATIONS

Beware of mob mentality and concealed weapons.

Some of them went there too, agitating the crowds and stirring them up. (Acts 17:13, NIV)

The assembly was in confusion: some were shouting one thing, some another. Most of the people did not even know why they were there. (Acts 19:32, NKJV)

So they rounded up some bad characters from the marketplace, formed a mob and started a riot in the city. (Acts 17:5, NIV)

His talk is smooth as butter, yet war is in his heart; his words are more soothing than oil, yet they are drawn swords. (Psalm 55:21, NIV)

EMERGENCIES

Practice does not make perfect. Perfect practice makes perfect.

And the LORD, he it is that does go before you; he will be with you, he will not fail you, neither forsake you: fear not, neither be dismayed. (Deuteronomy 31:8)

When you pass through the waters, I will be with you; And through the rivers, they shall not overflow you: When you walk through the fire, you shall not be burned; Neither shall the flame kindle upon you. (Isaiah 43:2-3)

Be of good courage, and he shall strengthen your heart. (Psalm 31:24)

The LORD is near unto all them that call upon him. (Psalm 145:18-19)

O Lord GOD, remember me, I pray thee, and strengthen me. (Judges 16:28)

Tackle every task that comes along, and if you fear God you can expect his blessing. (Ecclesiastes 9:18, TLB)

And be sure of this: I am with you always, even to the end of the age. (Matthew 28:20, NLT)

Be not overcome of evil, but overcome evil with good. (Romans 12:1)

For God hath not given us the spirit of fear; but of power, and of love, and of a sound mind. (2 Timothy 1:7)

Others were given great power in battle. (Hebrews 11:34)

EMERGENCIES

And God is able to make all grace abound toward you; that you, always having all sufficiency in all things, may abound to every good work. (2 Corinthians 9:8)

You have more than it takes.

And the LORD looked upon him, and said, Go in this your might. (Judges 6:14)

God is your strength and provider in all things, at all times, at any location.

And God said unto Moses, I AM THAT I AM. (Exodus 31:14)

ENERGY AND INDUSTRY

Photo courtesy of Walton County Sheriff Michael Adkinson

ENERGY AND INDUSTRY

If you have work to do, you might as well do your best.

A lazy man won't even dress the game he gets while hunting, but the diligent man makes good use of everything he finds. (Proverbs 12:27).

But they who wait for the LORD shall renew their strength; they shall mount up with wings like eagles; they shall run and not be weary; they shall walk and not faint. (Isaiah 40:31)

I even found great pleasure in hard work. (Ecclesiastes 2:10, TLB)

But it is good to be zealously affected always in a good thing. (Galatians 4:18)

Solomon seeing the young man that he was industrious, he made him ruler. (1 Kings 11:28).

Work willingly at whatever you do, as though you were working for the Lord rather than for people. Remember that the Lord will give you an inheritance as your reward, and that the Master you are serving is Christ. But if you do what is wrong, you will be paid back for the wrong you have done. (Colossians 3:23, NLT)

FAMILY

Photo courtesy of Houston Police Department

FAMILY

Children don't need your money. They need your time.

And, you fathers, provoke not your children to wrath: but bring them up in the nurture and admonition of the Lord. (Ephesians 6:4)

Fathers, provoke not your children to anger, lest they be discouraged. (Colossians 3:21)

Discipline your son in his early years while there is still hope. If you don't you will ruin his life. (Proverbs 19:18, TLB)

Help your children reach their own goals.

Having then gifts differing according to the grace that is given. (Romans 12:6)

A worthy wife is her husband's joy and crown. (Proverbs 12:4, TLB)

Charm can be deceptive and beauty doesn't last, but a woman who fears and reverences God shall be greatly praised. (Proverbs 31:30, TLB)

And I am sure of this, that he who began a good work in you will bring it to completion at the day of Jesus Christ. (Philippians 1:6)

But anyone who won't care for his own relatives when they need help, especially those living in his own family, has no right to say he is a Christian. Such a person is worse that the heathen. (1 Timothy 5:8, TLB).

For whosoever shall do the will of my Father which is in heaven, the same is my brother, and sister, and mother. (Matthew 12:50)

FINANCIAL MANAGEMENT

The way to wealth is as plain as the way to the mill: spend less than you earn. (Benjamin Franklin)

Honor the Lord by giving him the first part of all your income, and he will fill your barns. (Proverbs 3:9-10, TLB)

If you give to the poor, your needs will be supplied! (Proverbs 28:27, TLB)

Give generously, for your gifts will return to you later. (Ecclesiastes 11:1, TLB)

The wise store up choice food and olive oil, but fools gulp theirs down. (Proverbs 21:20, NIV)

Be not one of those who give pledges, who put up security for debts. If you have nothing with which to pay, why should your bed be taken from under you? (Proverbs 22:26-27, ESV).

Don't' weary yourself trying to get rich. Why waste you time? For riches can disappear as though they had wings of a bird. (Proverbs 23:4-5, TLB).

The man who wants to do right will get a rich reward. But the man who wants to get rich quick will quickly fail. (Proverbs 28:20, TLB)

Greed causes fighting; trusting God leads to prosperity. (Proverbs 28:25, TLB)

FINANCIAL MANAGEMENT

Give, and it shall be given unto you;
- **good measure,**
- **pressed down, and**
- **shaken together, and**
- **running over, shall men give into your bosom.**

For with the same measure that you mete withal it shall be measured to you again. (Luke 6:38)

Stay away from the love of money; be satisfied with what you have. For God has said, "I will never, never fail you nor forsake you." (Hebrews 13:5, TLB)

FRIENDS

Photo courtesy of Chief Stephen Carlisle, Roman Forest Police Department

FRIENDS

Your best friend is Jesus.

Draw nigh to God, and he will draw nigh to you. (James 4:8)

And there is a friend that sticks closer than a brother. (Proverbs 18:24)

He that walks with wise men shall be wise. (Proverbs 13:20a)

Don't visit your neighbor too often, or you will outwear your welcome! (Proverbs 25:17, TLB).

It's hard to soar with the eagles when you're surrounded by turkeys. Choose your friends as if your life depended on it.

Keep away from angry, short-tempered men, lest you learn to be like them and endanger your soul. (Proverbs 22:24-25, TLB)

Do not be misled: "Bad company corrupts good character." (1 Corinthians 15:33, NIV).

But a companion of fools shall be destroyed. (Proverbs 13:20b)

Don't associate with evil men; don't long for their favors and gifts. Their kindness is a trick; they want to use you as their pawn. The delicious food they serve will turn sour in your stomach and you will vomit it, and have to take back your words of appreciation for their "kindness." (Proverbs 23:6-8, TLB)

"My best friend is the one who brings out the best in me." - Abraham Lincoln

GRIEVING

Precious in the sight of the LORD is the death of his saints. (Psalm 116:15)

Yes, a wise man thinks much of death. (Ecclesiastes 7:4, TLB)

And devout men carried Stephen to his burial, and made great lamentation over him. (Acts 8:2)

A man might have a hundred children and live to be very old. But if he finds no satisfaction in life and doesn't even get a decent burial, it would have been better for him to be born dead. (Ecclesiastes 6:3, TLB)

And when all the congregation saw that Aaron was dead, they mourned for Aaron thirty days. (Numbers 20:29)

And in their death they were not divided: They were swifter than eagles, They were stronger than lions. (2 Samuel 1:23).

He heals the brokenhearted and binds up their wounds. (Psalm 147:3)

Weep with them that weep. (Romans 12:15).

Jesus wept. Then said the Jews, Behold how he loved him! (John 11:35–36)

And now, dear brothers and sisters, we want you to know what will happen to the believers who have died so you will not grieve like people who have no hope. For since we believe that Jesus died and was raised to life again, we also believe that when Jesus returns, God will bring back with him the believers who have died. (1 Thessalonians 4:13-14)

And God shall wipe away all tears from their eyes; and there shall be no more death, neither sorrow, nor crying, neither shall there be any more pain: for the former things are passed away. (Revelation 21:4).

Blessed are those who mourn, for they shall be comforted. (Matthew 5:4)

O death, where is your sting? O grave, where is your victory? (1 Corinthians 15:55)

But now he is dead, wherefore should I fast? Can I bring him back again? I shall go to him, but he shall not return to me. (2 Samuel 12:23)

I am the resurrection, and the life: he that believes in me, though he were dead, yet shall he live: (John 11:25)

For the Lord himself shall descend from heaven with a shout, with the voice of the archangel, and with the trump of God: and the dead in Christ shall rise first: Then we which are alive and remain shall be caught up together with them in the clouds, to meet the Lord in the air. (1 Thessalonians 4:16-17)

When my father and my mother forsake me, then the LORD will take me up. (Psalm 27:10)

We are confident, I say, and willing rather to be absent from the body, and to be present with the Lord. (2 Corinthians 5:8)

To appoint unto them that mourn in Zion,
To give unto them beauty for ashes,
The oil of joy for mourning,
The garment of praise for the spirit of heaviness;
That they might be called trees of righteousness,
The planting of the LORD, that he might be glorified. (Isaiah 61:3).

GRIEVING

I will not leave you orphans; I will come to you. (John 14:18, NKJV)

If you loved me, you would rejoice, because I said, I go unto the Father. (John 14:28)

For I am in a strait betwixt two, having a desire to depart, and to be with Christ; which is far better. (Philippians 1:23)

You shall guide me with your counsel, and afterward receive me to glory. (Psalm 73:24)

In my Father's house are many mansions: if it were not so, I would have told you. I go to prepare a place for you. And if I go and prepare a place for you, I will come again, and receive you unto myself; that where I am, there you may be also. (John 14:2,3)

Photo courtesy of Walton County Sheriff Michael Adkinson

GROWTH AND DEVELOPMENT

The more you know, the more you grow.

To learn you must want to be taught. (Proverbs 12:1, TLB)

An intelligent heart acquires knowledge, and the ear of the wise seeks knowledge. (Proverbs 18:15)

A king rejoices in servants who know what they are doing. (Proverbs 14:34, TLB)

If you refuse criticism you will end in poverty and disgrace: if you accept criticism you are on the road to fame. (Proverbs 15:1).

And I am sure of this, that he who began a good work in you will bring it to completion at the day of Jesus Christ. (Philippians 1:6)

I press on toward the goal for the prize of the upward call of God in Christ Jesus. (Philippians 3:14)

All Scripture is breathed out by God and profitable for teaching, for reproof, for correction, and for training in righteousness, that the man of God may be competent, equipped for every good work. (2 Timothy 3:16-17)

Photo courtesy of Walton County Sheriff Michael Adkinson

HAND-TO-HAND COMBAT

You are better trained than they are.

Praise the LORD, who is my rock. He trains my hands for war and gives my fingers skill for battle. (Psalm 144:1)

Be strong, and fight like men. (1 Samuel 4:9)

He slew two lion-like men of Moab: also he went down and slew a lion in a pit in a snowy day. (1 Chronicles 11:22)

In your strength I can crush an army. (Psalm 18:29, NLT)

HONESTY

You can make a good man able, but you can't make an able man good.

May integrity and honesty protect me. (Psalm 25:21, NLT)

The integrity of the upright guides them, but the crookedness of the treacherous destroys them. (Proverbs 11:3)

A good man's mind is filled with honest thoughts. (Proverbs 12:5, TLB)

Truth stands the test of time; lies are soon exposed. (Proverbs 12:19, TLB)

A good man hates lies; wicked men lie constantly and come to shame. (Proverbs 13:5, TLB)

Therefore, having put away falsehood, let each one of you speak the truth with his neighbor, for we are members one of another. (Ephesians 4:25)

Lying lips are an abomination to the LORD, but those who act faithfully are his delight. (Proverbs 12:22)

A wise man is hungry for truth, while the mocker feeds on trash. (Proverbs 15:14, TLB)

Better is a poor person who walks in his integrity than one who is crooked in speech and is a fool. (Proverbs 19:1)

Better to be poor and hones than rich and a cheater. (Proverbs 28:6, TLB)

HONESTY

Let what you say be simply 'Yes' or 'No'; anything more than this comes from evil. (Matthew 5:37)

In the end, people appreciate frankness more than flattery. (Proverbs 28:23, TLB)

HUMOR

**Want to hear a funny story?
Pull someone over for speeding.**

A merry heart does good like a medicine: but a broken spirit dries the bones. (Proverbs 17:22)

There is nothing better for a man, than that he should eat and drink, and that he should make his soul enjoy good in his labor. (Ecclesiastes 2:24)

A happy face means a glad heart; a sad face means a breaking heart. (Proverbs 15:13, TLB)

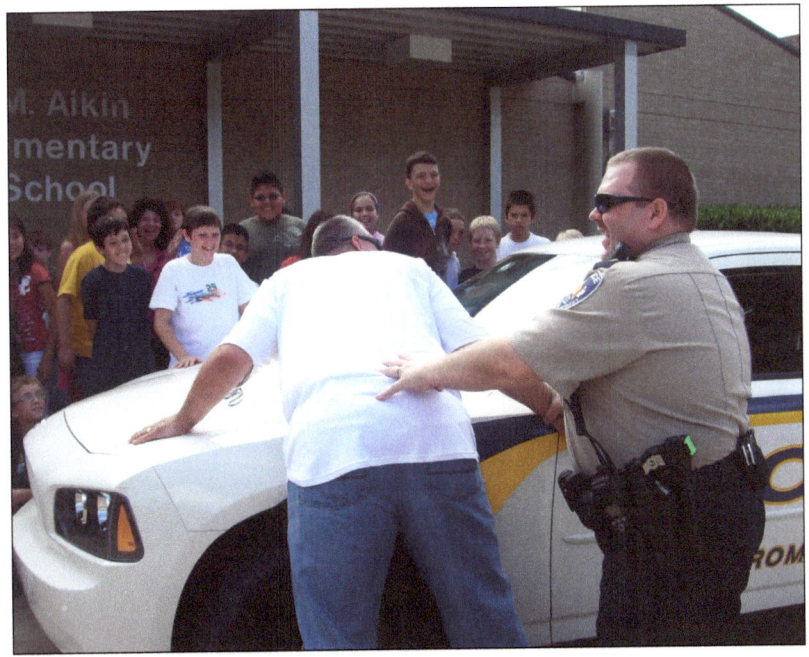

Photo courtesy of Chief Stephen Carlisle, Roman Forest Police Department

IMAGE

You are the face of the organization.

Man looks on the outward appearance, but the LORD looks on the heart. (1 Samuel 16:7)

So God created man in his own image, in the image of God created he him; male and female created he them. (Genesis 1:27)

They were swifter than eagles, they were stronger than lions. (2 Samuel 1:23).

Photo courtesy of Chief Stephen Carlisle, Roman Forest Police Department

INTERPERSONAL SKILLS

Find common ground and connect with them.

Therefore all things whatsoever you would that men should do to you, do you even so to them: for this is the law and the prophets. (Matthew 7:12)

Hatred stirs old quarrels, but love overlooks insults. (Proverbs 10:12)

A Soft answer turns away wrath, but harsh words cause quarrels. (Proverbs 15:1).

A man shall eat good by the fruit of his mouth: ... He that keeps his mouth keeps his life: But he that opens wide his lips shall have destruction. (Proverbs 13:2)

Self-control means controlling the tongue! A quick retort can ruin everything. (Proverbs 13:3)

A good man thinks before he speaks. (Proverbs 15:28).

A quick-tempered man starts fights; a cool-tempered man tries to stop them. (Proverbs 15:18)

How wonderful it is to say the right thing at the right time! (Proverbs 15:23, TLB)

A man that has friends must show himself friendly. (Proverbs 18:24).

As surely as a wind from the north brings cold, just as surely a retort causes anger! (Proverbs 25:23, TLB)

INTERPERSONAL SKILLS

Yanking a dog's ears is no more foolish than interfering in an argument that isn't any of your business. (Proverbs 26:17, TLB).

Fire goes out for lack of fuel, and tensions disappear when gossip stops. (Proverbs 26:20, TLB)

Flattery is a form of hatred and wounds cruelly. (Proverbs 26:28, TLB)

Open rebuke is better than secret love. Faithful are the wounds of a friend; But the kisses of an enemy are deceitful. (Proverbs 27:5–6).

As the churning of cream yields butter, and a blow to the nose causes bleeding, so anger causes quarrels. (Proverbs 30:33, TLB)

Whatsoever you would that men should do to you, do you even so to them. (Matthew 7:12)

Do nothing from rivalry or conceit, but in humility count others more significant than yourselves. (Philippians 2:3)

Love one another with brotherly affection. Outdo one another in showing honor. (Romans 12:9-10)

INTERROGATION

Many times, someone will tell you what happened.

Only simpletons believe everything they're told!
(Proverbs 14:15, NLT)

Punish false witnesses. Track down liars. (Proverbs 19:5, TLB)

A worthless witness cares nothing for the truth – he enjoys his sinning too much. (Proverbs 19: 28, TLB)

Give your servant therefore an understanding mind.
(1 Kings 3:9, ESV)

JUSTICE

JUSTICE

Those who administer justice should act justly.

Whoso sheds man's blood, by man shall his blood be shed: for in the image of God made he man. (Genesis 9:6)

He is the great and mighty God, the God of terror who shows no partiality and takes no bribes. (Deuteronomy 10:17, TLB).

We know that you are very honest and teach the truth regardless of the consequences, without fear or favor. (Matthew 22:17, TLB).

How short-sighted to fine the godly for being good! And to punish nobles for being honest! (Proverbs 17:26, TLB)

It is wrong for a judge to favor the wicked and condemn the innocent. (Proverbs 18:5, TLB)

What a shame – yes, how stupid! – to decide before knowing the facts! (Proverbs 18:13, TLB)

The Lord despises every kind of cheating. (Proverbs 20:10, TLB)

A wise king stamps out crime by severe punishment. (Proverbs 20:26, TLB)

Punishment that hurts chases evil from the heart. (Proverbs 20:30, TLB)

If a king is kind, honest and fair, his kingdom stands secure. (Proverbs 20:28, TLB)

When justice is done, it brings joy to the righteous but terror to evildoers. (Proverbs 21:15, NIV)

JUSTICE

The humble he guides in justice. (Psalm 25:9, NKJV)

The righteous care about justice for the poor, but the wicked have no such concern. (Proverbs 29:7, NIV)

You should defend those who cannot help themselves. Yes, speak up for the poor and needy and see that they get justice. (Proverbs 31:8, TLB)

For the LORD is a God of justice. Blessed are all who wait for him! … you will weep no more. How gracious he will be when you cry for help! As soon as he hears, he will answer you. (Isaiah 30:18-19, NIV)

Thus speaks the LORD of hosts, saying, Execute true judgment, and show mercy and compassions every man to his brother: and oppress not the widow, nor the fatherless, the stranger, nor the poor; and let none of you imagine evil against his brother in your heart. (Zechariah 7:9-10)

He has showed you, O man, what is good; and what does the LORD require of you, but to do justly, and to love mercy, and to walk humbly with thy God? (Micah 6:8)

God shows no partiality. (Acts 10:34, ESV)

Vengeance belongs unto me, I will recompense, says the Lord. And again, The Lord shall judge his people. (Hebrews 10:30).

And shall not God avenge his own elect, which cry day and night unto him, though he bear long with them? I tell you that he will avenge them speedily. Nevertheless when the Son of man comes, shall he find faith on the earth? (Luke 18:7-8)

Think of the innocent person, and watch the honest one. The man who has peace will have children to live after him. But sinners will be destroyed; in the end the wicked will die. (Psalm 37:37-38, NCV)

Hearken unto me, my people; and give ear unto me, O my nation: For a law shall proceed from me, and I will make my judgment to rest for a light of the people. My righteousness is near; my salvation is gone forth, and mine arms shall judge the people. (Isaiah 51:4-5)

LEADERSHIP

They don't care how much you know until they know how much you care. If you protect your officers, they will protect you. Success depends on good leaders.

With good men in authority, the people rejoice; but with the wicked in power, they groan. (Proverbs 29:2, TLB)

Moreover, look for able men from all the people, men who fear God, who are trustworthy and hate a bribe, and place such men over the people as chiefs of thousands, of hundreds, of fifties, and of tens. (Exodus 18:21)

Without wise leadership, a nation is in trouble; but with good counselors there is safety. (Proverbs 11:17, TLB)

Work hard and become a leader; be lazy and never succeed. (Proverbs 12:24, TLB).

Punish a mocker and others will learn from his example. Reprove a wise man and he will be the wiser. (Proverbs 19:25, TLB)

If they drink they may forget their duties and be unable to give justice to those who are oppressed. (Proverbs 31:4-5, TLB)

Oh, for a king who is devoted to his country! Only he can bring order from this chaos. (Ecclesiastes 5:9, TLB)

Because God does not punish sinners instantly, people feel it is safe to do wrong. (Ecclesiastes 8:11, TLB)

For God shows no partiality. (Romans 2:11, ESV)

LEADERSHIP

If God has given you administrative ability and put you in charge of the work of others, take the responsibility seriously.
(Romans 12:8, TLB)

Ask God to give you wisdom for leadership.

Give me now wisdom and knowledge, that I may go out and come in before this people: for who can judge this thy people, that is so great?
(2 Chronicles 1:10)

Photo courtesy of Chief Stephen Carlisle, Roman Forest Police Department

PARTNERS

❧

Be the partner you would like to have.

Wherever you go, I will go. (Ruth 1:16)

A word of encouragement does wonders! (Proverbs 12:25, TLB)

Iron sharpens iron, and one man sharpens another. (Proverbs 27:17)

Be with wise men and become wise. Be with evil me and become evil. (Proverbs 13:20, TLB)

Two are better than one, because they have a good reward for their toil. For if they fall, one will lift up his fellow. But woe to him who is alone when he falls and has not another to lift him up! (Ecclesiastes 4:9-10)

Let each of you look out not only for his own interests, but also for the interests of others. (Philippians 2:4, NKJV)

Therefore encourage one another and build one another up, just as you are doing. (1 Thessalonians 5:11).

PATROLLING

Be visible. Don't wait for trouble. An ounce of prevention is worth a ton of correction.

The LORD, before whom I walk, will send his angel with you, and prosper your way. (Genesis 24:40)

Be strong and courageous. Do not fear or be in dread of them, for it is the LORD your God who goes with you. He will not leave you or forsake you." (Deuteronomy 31:6, ESV)

The LORD shall preserve thy going out and thy coming in from this time forth, and even for evermore. (Psalm 121:8)

And behold, I am with you always. (Matthew 28:20)

Two are better than one, because they have a good reward for their toil. For if they fall, one will lift up his fellow. But woe to him who is alone when he falls and has not another to lift him up! (Ecclesiastes 4:9-10)

The heart of man plans his way, but the LORD establishes his steps. (Proverbs 16:9)

The eyes of the LORD are in every place, keeping watch on the evil and the good. (Proverbs 15:3)

Each labored on the work with one hand and held his weapon with the other. (Nehemiah 4:17)

Be watchful, stand firm in the faith, act like men, be strong. (1 Corinthians 16:13)

PATROLLING

But stay awake at all times, praying that you may have strength to escape all these things that are going to take place, and to stand before the Son of Man." (Luke 21:36).

It is dangerous and sinful to rush into the unknown. (Proverbs 19:2, TLB)

He guards you when you leave and when you return, he guards you now, he guards you always. (Psalm 121:8, The Message)

I will instruct you and teach you in the way you should go. (Psalm 32:8 NKJV)

Commit your way to the LORD; trust in him, and he will act. (Psalm 37:5)

Unless the LORD watches over the city, the watchman stays awake in vain. (Psalm 127:1)

Go and the LORD be with you. (1 Samuel 17:37)

Photo courtesy of Chief Stephen Carlisle, Roman Forest Police Department

PLANNING

Photo courtesy of Walton County Sheriff Michael Adkinson

PLANNING

The less you leave to chance, the better chance you have.

For which of you, intending to build a tower, sits not down first, and counts the cost, whether he have sufficient to finish it? (Luke 14:28)

It is pleasant to see plans develop. That is why fools refuse to give them up even when they are wrong. (Proverbs 12:5, TLB)

A wise man thinks ahead; a fool doesn't, and even brags about it! (Proverbs 13:16, TLB)

Those who plot evil shall wander away and be lost, but those who plan good shall be granted mercy and quietness. (Proverbs 14:13, TLB)

Plans go wrong with too few counselors; many counselors bring success. (Proverbs 15:22, TLB)

We can make our plans, but the final outcome is in God's hands. (Proverbs 16:1)

Commit your work to the LORD, and your plans will be established. (Proverbs 16:3, ESV)

We should make plans – counting on God to direct us. (Proverbs 16:9, TLB).

Though good advice lies deep within a counselor's heart, the wise man will draw it out. (Proverbs 20:5, TLB)

Any enterprise is built by wise planning, becomes strong through common sense, and profits wonderfully by keeping abreast of the facts. (Proverbs 24:3-4, TLB)

Be glad for all God is planning for you. (Romans 12:12, TLB)

POLICE DOGS

Long teeth and big noses.

The godly care for their animals. (Proverbs 12:10, NLT)

A living dog is better than a dead lion. (Ecclesiastes 9:4)

You, my people, will wash your feet in their blood, and even your dogs will get their share!" (Psalm 68:23, NLT)

Used with permission by John and Becki Johnston from AceK9.com.
Manufacturing life saving equipment for 30 years, honoring our heroes by capturing memorable moments.

POST TRAUMATIC STRESS DISORDER (PTSD)

There is no pit so deep that God cannot reach you.

God's name is I AM.
God is I AM safety when you need protection.
God is I AM calm when you face a storm.
God is I AM peace when you face stress.
God is I AM plenty when you need anything.
God is I AM the solution when you have a problem.
God is I AM clarity when you need understanding.

Casting all your care upon him, for He cares for you. (1 Peter 5:7, NKJV).

Your strength will come from settling down in complete dependence upon me. (Isaiah 30:16 The Message)

When I was upset and beside myself, you calmed me down and cheered me up. (Psalm 94:19, The Message)

The LORD is my shepherd; I shall not want. He restores my soul. (Psalm 23:1, 3)

He heals the broken in heart, and binds up their wounds. (Psalm 147:3)

He shall cover you with his feathers, and under his wings shall you trust. (Psalm 91:4)

POST TRAUMATIC STRESS DISORDER (PTSD)

Forget the former things; do not dwell on the past. (Isaiah 43:18, NIV).

When the enemy shall come in like a flood, The Spirit of the LORD shall lift up a standard against him. (Isaiah 59:19)

Ask God to calm the storms and lead you.

You have not, because you ask not. (James 4:2)

Behold, I have graven you upon the palms of my hands; your walls are continually before me. (Isaiah 49:16)

No weapon that is formed against you shall prosper. (Isaiah 54:17)

For I know the plans I have for you," says the LORD. "They are plans for good and not for disaster, to give you a future and a hope. In those days when you pray, I will listen. If you look for me wholeheartedly, you will find me. (Jeremiah 29: 11-13)

Yes, I have loved you with an everlasting love: Therefore with loving kindness have I drawn you. Again I will build you, and you shall be built ... and shall go forth in the dances of them that make merry. (Jeremiah 31:3-4)

PRAYER

The One who created the ear is not deaf.

Then shall you call upon me, and you shall go and pray unto me, and I will hearken unto you. And you shall seek me, and find me, when you shall search for me with all your heart. (Jeremiah 29:12–13)

For the eyes of the Lord are on the righteous, and his ears are open to their prayer. (1 Peter 3:11)

*Ask, and it will be given to you; seek, and you will find; knock, and it will be opened to you. For everyone who asks receives, and he who seeks finds, and to him who knocks it will be opened.
(Matthew 7:7-8, NKJV)*

Some prayer, some power. Much prayer, much power.

And this is the confidence that we have in him, that, if we ask any thing according to his will, he hears us: And if we know that he hears us, whatsoever we ask, we know that we have the petitions that we desired of him. (1 John 5:14-15)

PREPARATION

Preparation is the secret of life.

If you won't plow in the cold, you won't eat at the harvest. (Proverbs 20:4, TLB)

Go ahead and prepare for the conflict, but victory comes from God. (Proverbs 21:31)

A prudent man foresees the difficulties ahead and prepares for them; the simpleton goes blindly on and suffers the consequences. (Proverbs 22:3)

Study to show yourself approved. (2 Timothy 2:15)

Complete armor provides complete protection. Partial armor provides partial protection.

Put on the whole armor. (Ephesians 6:11)

Be strong, and fight like men (1 Samuel 4:9)

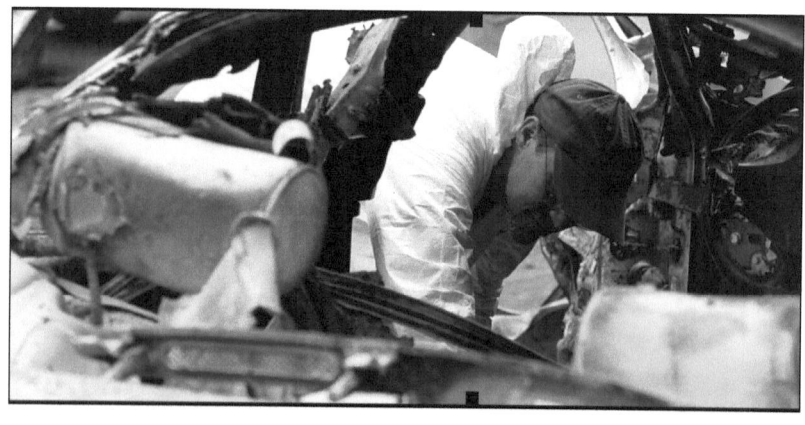

PREVENTING SUICIDE

The Lord has given me his words of wisdom so that I may know what I should say to all these weary ones. (Isaiah 50:4, TLB)

Rejoice in hope, be patient in tribulation, be constant in prayer. (Romans 12:12, ESV)

Weep with those who weep. (Romans 12:15 NASB)

He comforts us in all our troubles so that we can comfort others. When they are troubled, we will be able to give them the same comfort God has given us. (2 Corinthians 1:4, NLT)

Therefore encourage one another and build one another up. (1 Thessalonians 5:10, ESV)

PROMOTION TO HIGHER RESPONSIBILITY

Photo courtesy of Walton County Sheriff Michael Adkinson

PROMOTION TO HIGHER RESPONSIBILITY

Promotion gives you the opportunity to help more people.

Much is required from those to whom much is given, for their responsibility is greater. (Luke 12:48, TLB)

Work hard and become a leader; be lazy and never succeed. (Proverbs 12:24)

Better a little with reverence for God, than great treasure and trouble with it. (Proverbs 15:16, TLB).

Let the people praise you, O God; Let all the people praise you. Then shall the earth yield her increase; and God, even our own God, shall bless us. God shall bless us. (Psalm 67:5-7)

One who is faithful in a very little is also faithful in much, and one who is dishonest in a very little is also dishonest in much. If then you have not been faithful in the unrighteous wealth, who will entrust to you the true riches? And if you have not been faithful in that which is another's, who will give you that which is your own? (Luke 16:10-12)

Blessings on you if I return and find you faithfully doing your work. I will put such faithful ones in charge of everything I own! (Matthew 2546-47, TLB)

Humble yourselves in the sight of the Lord, and he shall lift you up. (James 4:10).

PROTECTING THE WEAK

Want to feel great? Help someone in need.

Give generously, for your gifts will return to you later. Divide your gifts among many, for in the days ahead you yourself may need much help. (Ecclesiastes 11:1-2, TLB)

A happy face means a glad heart; a sad face means a breaking heart. (Proverbs 15:13, TLB)

Neglect is a form of child abuse.

But if any provide not for his own, and especially for those of his own house, he has denied the faith, and is worse than an infidel. (1 Timothy 5:8)

And a person's enemies will be those of his own household. (Matthew 10:36, ESV)

Speak up for those who cannot speak for themselves; ensure justice for those being crushed. (Proverbs 31:8)

You shall not afflict any widow, or fatherless child. (Exodus 22:22)

Learn to do right; seek justice. Defend the oppressed. Take up the cause of the fatherless; plead the case of the widow. (Isaiah 1:17, NIV)

PROTECTING THE WEAK

Woe unto them that decree unrighteous decrees,
And that write grievousness which they have prescribed;
To turn aside the needy from judgment,
And to take away the right from the poor of my people,
That widows may be their prey,
And that they may rob the fatherless! (Isaiah 10:1-2)

You will bring justice to the orphans and the oppressed, so mere people can no longer terrify them. (Psalm 10:18, NLT)

Give justice to the poor and the orphan; uphold the rights of the oppressed and the destitute. (Psalm 82:3, NLT).

I am the good shepherd: the good shepherd gives his life for the sheep. But he that is an hireling, and not the shepherd, whose own the sheep are not, sees the wolf coming, and leaves the sheep, and flees: and the wolf catches them, and scatters the sheep. The hireling flees, because he is an hireling, and cares not for the sheep. (John 10:11-14)

He heals the broken in heart, and binds up their wounds. (Psalm 147:3)

Reference:
http://www.joyfulheartfoundation.org/learn/child-abuse-neglect/effects-child-abuse-neglect

PROTECTION

Used with permission by John and Becki Johnston from AceK9.com.
Manufacturing life saving equipment for 30 years, honoring our heroes by capturing memorable moments.

PROTECTION

Complete armor provides complete protection. Partial armor provides partial protection.

Put on the whole armor. (Ephesians 6:11)

Keep me as the apple of the eye, Hide me under the shadow of your wings. (Psalm 17:8)

The LORD shall preserve your going out and your coming in from this time forth, and even for evermore. (Psalm 121:8)

As the mountains surround Jerusalem, so the Lord surrounds his people, from this time forth and forevermore. (Psalm 125:2)

PSALM 23
The LORD is my shepherd; I shall not want.
He makes me to lie down in green pastures:
He leads me beside the still waters.
He restores my soul:
He leads me in the paths of righteousness for his name's sake.
Yes, though I walk through the valley of the shadow of death,
I will fear no evil: for you are with me;
Your rod and your staff they comfort me.
You prepare a table before me in the presence of my enemies:
You anoint my head with oil; my cup runs over.
Surely goodness and mercy shall follow me all the days of my life:
And I will dwell in the house of the LORD for ever. (23rd Psalm)

PROTECTION

PSALM 91
He that dwells in the secret place of the most High
Shall abide under the shadow of the Almighty.
I will say of the LORD, He is my refuge and my fortress:
My God; in him will I trust.
Surely he shall deliver you from the snare of the fowler,
And from the noisome pestilence.
He shall cover you with his feathers,
And under his wings shall you trust:
His truth shall be your shield and buckler.
You shall not be afraid for the terror by night;
Nor for the arrow that flies by day;
Nor for the pestilence that walks in darkness;
Nor for the destruction that wastes at noonday.
A thousand shall fall at thy side,
And ten thousand at thy right hand;
But it shall not come near you.
Only with your eyes shall you behold
And see the reward of the wicked.
Because you have made the LORD, which is my refuge,
Even the most High, your habitation;
There shall no evil befall you,
Neither shall any plague come near your dwelling.
For he shall give his angels charge over you,
To keep you in all your ways.
They shall bear you up in their hands,
Lest you dash your foot against a stone.
You shall tread upon the lion and adder:
The young lion and the dragon shall you trample under feet.
Because he has set his love upon me, therefore will I deliver him:
I will set him on high, because he has known my name.
He shall call upon me, and I will answer him:
I will be with him in trouble;
I will deliver him, and honor him.
With long life will I satisfy him,
And show him my salvation. (Psalm 91)

PROTECTION

The LORD is my shepherd; I shall not want.
He makes me to lie down in green pastures:
He leads me beside the still waters.
He restores my soul:
He leads me in the paths of righteousness for his name's sake.
Yes, though I walk through the valley of the shadow of death,
I will fear no evil: for you are with me;
Your rod and your staff comfort me.
You prepare a table before me in the presence of my enemies:
You anoint my head with oil; my cup runs over.
Surely goodness and mercy shall follow me all the days of my life:
And I will dwell in the house of the LORD for ever. (Psalm 23)

Ask God to calm the storms and lead you.
You have not, because you ask not. (James 4:2)

Behold, I have graven you upon the palms of my hands;
Your walls are continually before me. (Isaiah 49:16)

No weapon that is formed against you shall prosper;
And every tongue that shall rise against you in judgment you shall condemn. This is the heritage of the servants of the LORD,
And their righteousness is of me, says the LORD. (Isaiah 54:17)

Fear not, for I am with you; be not dismayed, for I am your God; I will strengthen you, I will help you, I will uphold you with my righteous right hand. (Isaiah 41:10)

Photo courtesy of Walton County Sheriff Michael Adkinson

PROVISION

Photo courtesy of Chief Stephen Carlisle, Roman Forest Police Department

PROVISION

**You'll do fine if you stay on the Vine.
God owns everything. It won't strain him to provide for you one more day.**

I am the vine, you are the branches: He that abides in me, and I in him, the same brings forth much fruit: for without me you can do nothing. (John 15:5)

But seek first the kingdom of God, and his righteousness; and all these things shall be added unto you. (Matthew 6:33)

But my God shall supply all your need according to his riches in glory by Christ Jesus. (Philippians 4:19)

My cup runs over. (Psalm 23:5)

The young lions do lack, and suffer hunger: But they that seek the LORD shall not want any good thing. (Psalm 34:10)

Delight yourself in the LORD, and he will give you the desires of your heart. (Psalm 37:4, ESV)

Then shall you delight yourself in the LORD; And I will cause you to ride upon the high places of the earth. (Isaiah 58:14).

You have not, because you ask not. (James 4:2)

RECOGNIZING ELDER ABUSE

RECOGNIZING ELDER ABUSE

⚜

Abuse of older people can take several forms: financial, emotional, physical, intellectual, and spiritual. Talk to the potential victims in person.

A person's enemies will be those of his own household. (Matthew 10:36, ESV)

For men shall be lovers of their own selves, covetous, boasters, proud, blasphemers, disobedient to parents, unthankful, unholy, Without natural affection, trucebreakers, false accusers, incontinent, fierce, despisers of those that are good, traitors, heady, high-minded, lovers of pleasures more than lovers of God. (2 Timothy 3:2-5)

But if any provide not for his own, and especially for those of his own house, he has denied the faith, and is worse than an infidel. (1 Timothy 5:8)

Speak up for those who cannot speak for themselves; ensure justice for those being crushed. (Proverbs 31:8)

A wise son hears his father's instruction: But a scorner hears not rebuke. (Proverbs 13:1)

Cursed is anyone who despises his father or mother. (Deuteronomy 27:16, TLB).

The eye that mocks at his father, and despises to obey his mother, The ravens of the valley shall pick it out, and the young eagles shall eat it. (Proverbs 30:17)

RECOVERING STOLEN PROPERTY

RECOVERING STOLEN PROPERTY

Right the wrong.

He recovered all the goods. (Genesis 14:16, NIV)

Have not I commanded you? Be strong and of a good courage; be not afraid, neither be you dismayed: for the LORD your God is with you wherever you go. (Joshua 1:9)

A gracious woman retains honor: and strong men retain riches. (Proverbs 11:16)

If a man gives to his neighbor money or goods to keep safe, and it is stolen from the man's house, then, if the thief is found, he shall pay double. (Exodus 22:7, ESV)

The LORD spoke to Moses, saying, "If anyone sins and commits a breach of faith against the LORD by deceiving his neighbor in a matter of deposit or security, or through robbery, or if he has oppressed his neighbor or has found something lost and lied about it, swearing falsely—in any of all the things that people do and sin thereby— if he has sinned and has realized his guilt and will restore what he took by robbery or what he got by oppression or the deposit that was committed to him or the lost thing that he found or anything about which he has sworn falsely, he shall restore it in full and shall add a fifth to it, and give it to him to whom it belongs on the day he realizes his guilt. (Leviticus 6:1-7, ESV)

RECRUITING

Good people are getting harder to find.

An employer who hires a fool or a bystander is like an archer who shoots at random. (Proverbs 26:10, NLT)

Man looks on the outward appearance, but the LORD looks on the heart. (1 Samuel 16:7)

Photo courtesy of Walton County Sheriff Michael Adkinson

RELIABILITY

Your word is your bond.

God delights in those who keep their promises, and abhors those who don't. (Proverbs 12:22, TLB)

See a man diligent in his business? He shall stand before kings; He shall not stand before mean men. (Proverbs 22:29)

The wise man will find a time and a way to do what he says. (Ecclesiastes 8:5, TLB)

He that is faithful in that which is least is faithful also in much: and he that is unjust in the least is unjust also in much. If therefore you have not been faithful in the unrighteous mammon, who will commit to your trust the true riches? And if you have not been faithful in that which is another man's, who shall give you that which is your own? (Luke 16:10–12).

Photo courtesy of Chief Stephen Carlisle, Roman Forest Police Department

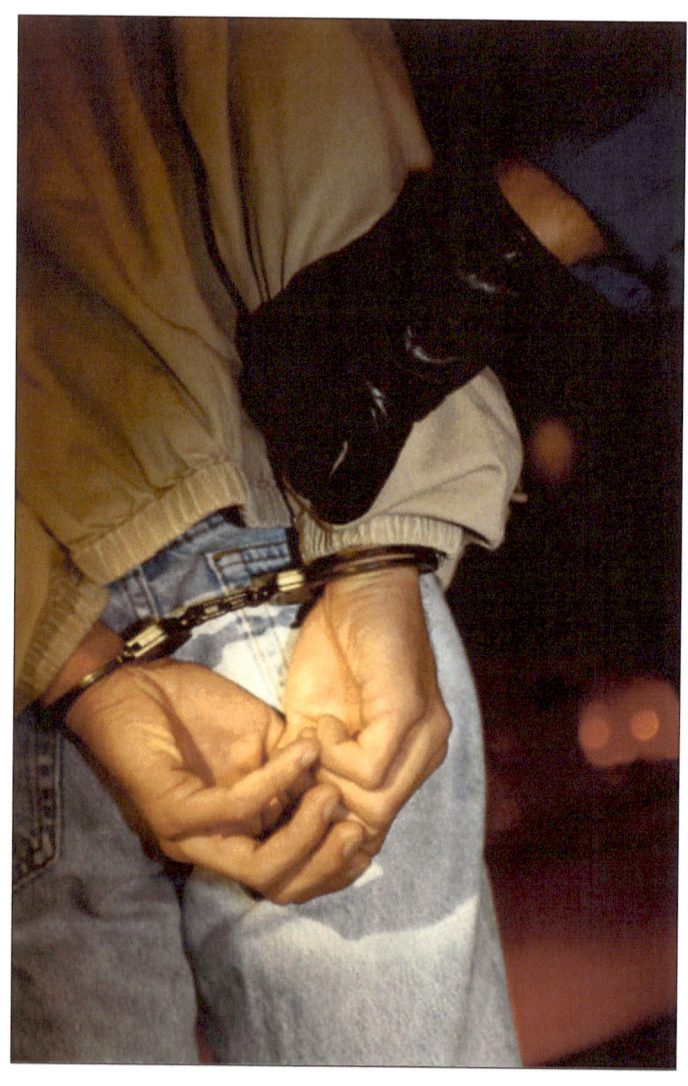

REMEMBERING CRIME VICTIMS

Everyone is created in God's image and has dignity.

And God said, Let us make man in our image, after our likeness. (Genesis 1:26)

The Christian who is pure and without fault, from God the Father's point of view, is the one who takes care of orphans and widows, and who remains true to the Lord – not soiled or dirtied by his contacts with the world . (James 1:27, TLB)

*Suppose you see a brother or sister who has no food or clothing, and you say, "Good-bye and have a good day; stay warm and eat well"—but then you don't give that person any food or clothing. What good does that do? So you see, faith by itself isn't enough.
(James 2:15-17, NLT)*

Remember, it is sin to know what you ought to do and then not do it. (James 4:17, NLT)

*Therefore encourage one another and build up one another.
(1 Thessalonians 5:11, ASV)*

*The Lord GOD has given me the tongue of the learned, that I should know how to speak a word in season to him that is weary.
(Isaiah 50:4)*

Weep with them that weep. (Romans 12:15)

*Withhold not good from them to whom it is due, when it is in the power of your hand to do it.
Say not unto thy neighbor, go, and come again, and tomorrow I will give; when you have it by you. (Proverbs 3:27-28)*

REPORTING

REPORTING

The department needs true, accurate, and complete information to take sound action.

You shall not raise a false report: put not your hand with the wicked to be an unrighteous witness. (Exodus 23:1)

Get the facts at any price. (Proverbs 23:23, TLB)

Make it plain. (Habakkuk 2:2)

And she said to the king, It was a true report that I heard (1 Kings 10:6)

And I took unto me faithful witnesses to record. (Isaiah 8:2)

For my mouth shall speak truth; and wickedness is an abomination to my lips. (Proverbs 8:7)

He that speaks truth shows forth righteousness: but a false witness deceit. (Proverbs 12:17)

The lip of truth shall be established for ever: but a lying tongue is but for a moment. (Proverbs 12:19)

That which was written was upright, even words of truth. (Ecclesiastes 12:10)

Lie not one to another. (Colossians 3:9)

REPUTATION

Conduct yourself appropriately. It's hard to un-ring a bell.

If your goals are good, you will be respected. (Proverbs 11:27, GNT)

Before honor is humility. (Proverbs 15:33)

If you must choose, take a good name rather than great riches. (Proverbs 22:1, TLB).

Dead flies will cause even a bottle of perfume to stink! Yes, a small mistake can outweigh much wisdom and honor. (Ecclesiastes 10:1, TLB)

Photo courtesy of Chief Stephen Carlisle, Roman Forest Police Department

REST

**Even Jesus made time to rest.
Sometimes the most spiritual thing you can do is rest.**

*And he withdrew himself into the wilderness, and prayed.
(Luke 5:16)*

And on the seventh day God ended his work which he had made; and he rested on the seventh day from all his work which he had made. And God blessed the seventh day, and sanctified it: because that in it he had rested from all his work which God created and made. (Genesis 2:2-3)

I have said these things to you, that in me you may have peace. In the world you will have tribulation. But take heart; I have overcome the world." (John 16:33)

*Casting all your anxieties on him, because he cares for you.
(1 Peter 5:7)*

It is vain for you to rise up early, to sit up late, to eat the bread of sorrows: For so he gives his beloved sleep. (Psalm 127:2)

SERGEANTS, LIEUTENANTS, AND CAPTAINS

✠

Believe it or not, God put them there to help you. Support the chain-of-command.

Be subject for the Lord's sake to every human institution. (1 Peter 2:13)

Hidden in the hands of Moses and Aaron, You led your people like a flock of sheep. (Psalm 77:20, The Message)

Would you have no fear of the one who is in authority? Then do what is good, and you will receive his approval, for he is God's servant for your good. But if you do wrong, be afraid, for he does not bear the sword in vain. (Romans 13: 11-14)

If God has given you administrative ability and put you in charge of the work of others, take the responsibility seriously. (Romans 12:8, TLB)

Those who obey him will not be punished. (Ecclesiastes 8:5, TLB)

If the boss is angry with you, don't quit! A quiet spirit will quiet his bad temper. (Ecclesiastes 10:4, TLB)

Be submissive to rulers and authorities, to be obedient, to be ready for every good work. (Titus 3:1)

Obey your leaders and submit to them, for they are keeping watch over your souls, as those who will have to give an account. Let them do this with joy and not with groaning, for that would be of no advantage to you. (Hebrews 13:17, ESV).

SERGEANTS, LIEUTENANTS, AND CAPTAINS

Keep your mouth closed and you will stay out of trouble. (Proverbs 21:23, TLB)

They must not talk back, nor steal, but must show themselves to be entirely trustworthy. (Titus 2:9-10, TLB)

Do not grow weary in doing good. (2 Thessalonians 3:13)

No man that wars entangles himself with the affairs of this life; that he may please him who has chosen him to be a soldier. (2 Timothy 2:4).

Seize the initiative. Don't wait to be told to take action.

I exhort therefore, that, first of all, supplications, prayers, intercessions, and giving of thanks, be made for all men; For kings, and for all that are in authority; that we may lead a quiet and peaceable life in all godliness and honesty. (1 Timothy 2:1–2)

SET THE EXAMPLE

Photo courtesy of Chief Stephen Carlisle, Roman Forest Police Department

SET THE EXAMPLE

People need good, visible examples.

So that you were examples to all. (1 Thessalonians 1:7)

Be followers together of me, and mark them which walk so as you have us for an example. (Philippians 3:17).

And what you have heard from me in the presence of many witnesses entrust to faithful men who will be able to teach others also. (2 Timothy 2:2)

Show yourself in all respects to be a model of good works, and in your teaching show integrity, dignity, and sound speech that cannot be condemned, so that an opponent may be put to shame, having nothing evil to say about us. (Titus 2:7-8)

I will show you my faith by my works (James 2:18)

By this we know love, because He laid down His life for us. And we also ought to lay down our lives for the brethren. (1 John 3:16)

SPECIAL WEAPONS AND TACTICS (SWAT)

SPECIAL WEAPONS AND TACTICS (SWAT)

The violent take it by force. (Matthew 11:12).

The LORD is with you, O mighty man of valor. (Judges 6:12, ESV)

You shall rise up from the ambush, and seize upon the city: for the LORD your God will deliver it into your hand. (Joshua 8:7)

They were experts with both shield and spear and were "lion-faced men, swift as deer upon the mountains." (1 Chronicles 12:19, TLB)

Blessed be the LORD my strength, which teaches my hands to war. (Psalm 144:1)

Children in whom was no blemish, but well favored, and skilful in all wisdom, and cunning in knowledge, and understanding science. (Daniel 1:4)

There be three things which go well, Yes, four are comely in going: A lion which is strongest among beasts, and turns not away for any. (Proverbs 30:29-30)

Men who have risked their lives. (Acts 15:26, NIV)

I am sending you out like sheep among wolves. Therefore be as shrewd as snakes. (Matthew 10:16, NIV)

For the weapons of our warfare are not carnal, but mighty through God to the pulling down of strong holds. (2 Corinthians 10:4)

SUPERVISION

Photo courtesy of Walton County Sheriff Michael Adkinson

SUPERVISION

It's all about leadership.

Throw out the mocker, and you will be rid of tension, fighting and quarrels. (Proverbs 22:10, TLB).

Don't waste your breath on a rebel. He will despise the wisest advice. (Proverbs 23:9, TLB).

To trust a rebel to convey a message is as foolish as cutting off your feet and drinking poison! (Proverbs 26:6, TLB)

The master may get better work from an untrained apprentice than from a skilled rebel! (Proverbs 26:10, TLB)

With honest, sensible leaders there is stability. (Proverbs 28:2, TLB)

A wicked ruler is as dangerous to the poor as a lion or bear attacking them. (Proverbs 28:15, TLB)

If God has given you administrative ability and put you in charge of the work of others, take the responsibility seriously. (Romans 12:8, TLB)

For the Lord's sake, submit to all human authority—whether the king as head of state, or the officials he has appointed. For the king has sent them to punish those who do wrong and to honor those who do right. (1 Peter 2:13-14, NLT)

Keep these rules without prejudging, doing nothing from partiality. (1 Timothy 5:21, ESV)

TEAMWORK

TEAMWORK

If everyone does his or her part, the team will be successful.

A word of encouragement does wonders! (Proverbs 12:25, TLB)

Iron sharpens iron, and one man sharpens another. (Proverbs 27:17)

Be with wise men and become wise. Be with evil me and become evil. (Proverbs 13:20, TLB)

*Two are better than one, because they have a good reward for their toil. For if they fall, one will lift up his fellow. But woe to him who is alone when he falls and has not another to lift him up! Again, if two lie together, they keep warm, but how can one keep warm alone? And though a man might prevail against one who is alone, two will withstand him—a threefold cord is not quickly broken.
(Ecclesiastes 4:9)*

Therefore encourage one another and build one another up, just as you are doing. (1 Thessalonians 5:11).

TEMPTATION

Photo courtesy of Chief Stephen Carlisle, Roman Forest Police Department

TEMPTATION

A short season of pleasure is not worth the ensuing heartache.

Choosing rather to suffer affliction with the people of God, than to enjoy the pleasures of sin for a season. (Hebrews 11:25)

Sin lies at the door (Genesis 4:7)

Ill-gotten gain brings no lasting happiness; right living does. (Proverbs 10:2)

Wealth from gambling quickly disappears; wealth from hard work grows. (Proverbs 13:11)

It is wrong to accept a bribe to twist justice. (Proverbs 17:23, TLB).

And you shall take no bribe, for a bribe blinds the clear-sighted and subverts the cause of those who are in the right. (Exodus 23:8, ESV)

Dishonest money brings grief to all the family, but hating bribes brings happiness. (Proverbs 15:27, TLB)

Sexual sin often starts with the eyes. However, flattery is also deadly.

A prostitute is a dangerous trap; those cursed of God are caught in it. (Proverbs 22:14, TLB).

For a whore is a deep ditch; And a strange woman is a narrow pit. (Proverbs 23:27, TLB).

TEMPTATION

Wine gives false courage; hard liquor leads to brawls; what fools men are to let it master them, making them reel drunkenly down the street! (Proverbs 20:1, TLB)

Who has sorrow? Who has contentions? who has babbling? Who has wounds without cause? Who has redness of eyes? They that tarry long at the wine; They that go to seek mixed wine... At the last it bites like a serpent, And stings like an adder. (Proverbs 23:29–32).

Dishonest gain will never last, so why take the risk? (Proverbs 21:6, TLB)

If you think you are standing strong, be careful not to fall. The temptations in your life are no different from what others experience. And God is faithful. He will not allow the temptation to be more than you can stand. When you are tempted, he will show you a way out so that you can endure. (1 Corinthians 10:12–13, NLT)

It's easier to die to sin than to struggle against it.

I am crucified with Christ: nevertheless I live; yet not I, but Christ lives in me: and the life which I now live in the flesh I live by the faith of the Son of God, who loved me, and gave himself for me. (Galatians 2:20)

Looking unto Jesus the author and finisher of our faith; who for the joy that was set before him endured the cross, despising the shame. (Hebrews 12:2)

TERRORISM

❧

God confronts the evil of each generation.

He that dwells in the secret place of the most High
Shall abide under the shadow of the Almighty.
I will say of the LORD, He is my refuge and my fortress:
My God; in him will I trust.
Surely he shall deliver you from the snare of the fowler,
And from the noisome pestilence.
He shall cover you with his feathers,
And under his wings shall you trust:
His truth shall be your shield and buckler.
You shall not be afraid for the terror by night;
Nor for the arrow that flies by day;
Nor for the pestilence that walks in darkness;
Nor for the destruction that wastes at noonday.
A thousand shall fall at your side,
And ten thousand at your right hand;
But it shall not come near you. (Psalm 91:1-7)

In righteousness shall you be established:
You shall be far from oppression; for you shall not fear:
And from terror; for it shall not come near you. (Isaiah 54:14)

Don't be afraid of those who can kill only your bodies – but can't touch your souls! Fear only God who can destroy both soul and body in hell. Not one sparrow (What do they cost? Two for a penny?) can fall to the ground without your Father knowing it. And the very hairs of your head are all numbered. So don't worry! You are more valuable to him than many sparrows. (Matthew 10:28-31)

Be sober, be vigilant; because your adversary the devil, as a roaring lion, walks about, seeking whom he may devour. (1 Peter 5:8)

Because the LORD revealed their plot to me, I knew it, for at that time he showed me what they were doing. (Jeremiah 11:18, NIV)

Greater is he that is in you, than he that is in the world. (1 John 4:4)

TESTIFYING

Photo courtesy of Walton County Sheriff Michael Adkinson

TESTIFYING

Testify. Don't opinionate.

And do not slant your testimony in favor of a person just because that person is poor. (Exodus 23:3, NLT).

You shall do no injustice in court. You shall not be partial to the poor or defer to the great, but in righteousness shall you judge your neighbor. (Leviticus 19:15, ESV)

Lying lips are abomination to the LORD. (Proverbs 12:22)

A faithful witness will not lie: But a false witness will utter lies. (Proverbs 14:5)

A true witness delivers souls: But a deceitful witness speaketh lies. (Proverbs 14:25)

Listen before you answer. If you don't you are being stupid and insulting. (Proverbs 18:13, GNT).

But if any of you needs wisdom, you should ask God for it. He is generous and enjoys giving to all people, so he will give you wisdom. (James 1:5, NCV).

But above all things, my brethren, swear not, neither by heaven, neither by the earth, neither by any other oath: **but let your yes be yes; and your no, no;** *lest you fall into condemnation. (James 5:12)*

TOUGH TIMES

Photo courtesy of Walton County Sheriff Michael Adkinson

TOUGH TIMES

**When trouble comes, people may walk away.
But God draws near to you.**

If God be for us, who can be against us? (Romans 8:31)

Shall we receive only pleasant things from the hand of God and never anything unpleasant? (Job 2:10)

But I say unto you, Love your enemies, bless them that curse you, do good to them that hate you, and pray for them which despitefully use you, and persecute you; That you may be the children of your Father which is in heaven: for he makes his sun to rise on the evil and on the good, and sends rain on the just and on the unjust. For if you love them which love you, what reward have you? do not even the publicans the same? (Matthew 5:44-46)

If you faint in the day of adversity, your strength is small. (Proverbs 24:10)

Many are the afflictions of the righteous: But the LORD delivers him out of them all. (Psalm 34:19)

God is our refuge and strength, always ready to help in times of trouble. (Psalm 46:1)

Resist the devil and he will flee from you. Draw near to God and he will draw near to you. (James 4:7-8)

The Lord rebuke thee. (Jude 9)

Therefore, put on every piece of God's armor so you will be able to resist the enemy in the time of evil. Then after the battle you will still be standing firm. Stand your ground. (Ephesians 6:13-14, NLT)

TOUGH TIMES

For I am persuaded, that neither death, nor life, nor angels, nor principalities, nor powers, nor things present, nor things to come, nor height, nor depth, nor any other creature, shall be able to separate us from the love of God, which is in Christ Jesus our Lord.
(Romans 8:38-39)

Keep your eyes on Jesus, our leader and instructor. He was willing to die a shameful death on the cross because of the joy he knew would be his afterwards; and now he sits in the place of honor by the throne of God. If you want to keep from becoming fainthearted and weary, think about his patience. (Hebrews 12:2-3, TLB)

But the God of all grace, who has called us unto his eternal glory by Christ Jesus, after that you have suffered a while, make you perfect, establish, strengthen, settle you. (1 Peter 5:10)

And we know that for those who love God all things work together for good, for those who are called according to his purpose. (Romans 8:28, ESV)

For I know the thoughts that I think toward you, says the LORD, thoughts of peace, and not of evil, to give you an expected end. (Jeremiah 29:11)

I called upon the LORD in distress: The LORD answered me, and set me in a large place. The LORD is on my side; I will not fear: What can man do unto me? (Psalm 118:5-6)

A friend loves at all times, and a brother is born for adversity. (Proverbs 17:17)

When we consider God's power and wisdom, our problems are small.
David encouraged himself in the LORD his God. (1 Samuel 30:6)

For which cause we faint not; but though our outward man perish, yet the inward man is renewed day by day. For our light affliction, which is but for a moment, works for us a far more exceeding and eternal weight of glory. (2 Corinthians 4:16-18)

These things I have spoken unto you, that in me you might have peace. In the world you shall have tribulation: but be of good cheer; I have overcome the world. (John 16:33)

TRAFFIC CONTROL

Take charge of the situation and maintain control.

For God is not the author of confusion. (1 Corinthians 14:33)

For if the trumpet give an uncertain sound, who shall prepare himself? (1 Corinthians 14:8)

Lift up thy voice with strength. (Isaiah 40:9)

I will instruct you and teach you in the way which you shall go: I will guide you with my eye. (Psalm 32:8).

So he ...guided them by the skillfulness of his hands. (Psalm 78:72)

But when he saw the multitudes, he was moved with compassion on them, because they fainted, and were scattered abroad, as sheep having no shepherd. (Matthew 9:36)

TRAINING

All the knowledge in the world doubles every two months. Specialize and stay current.

Give instruction to a wise man, and he will be yet wiser: Teach a just man, and he will increase in learning. (Proverbs 9:9)

A wise teacher makes learning a joy. (Proverbs 15:2).

For precept must be upon precept, precept upon precept; Line upon line, line upon line; Here a little, and there a little. (Isaiah 28:10)

If you have run with the footmen, and they have wearied you, then how can you contend with horses? and if in the land of peace, wherein you trust, they wearied thee, then how will you do in the swelling of Jordan? (Jeremiah 12:5, TLB)

That the man of God may be competent, equipped for every good work. (2 Timothy 3:16, ESV)

Blessed be the LORD, my rock, who trains my hands for war, and my fingers for battle. (Psalm 144:1, ESV)

TRAINING

Photo courtesy of Chief Stephen Carlisle, Roman Forest Police Department

WORK

Work is good. Wasting time talking is bad.

He also that is slothful in his work is brother to him that is a great waster. (Proverbs 18:9)

Be you strong therefore, and let not your hands be weak: for your work shall be rewarded. (2 Chronicles 15:7).

Tell the people to get moving! (Exodus 14:15, NLT)

If you love sleep, you will end in poverty. Stay awake, work hard, and there will be plenty to eat! (Proverbs 20:13, TLB)

If any would not work, neither should he eat. (2 Thessalonians 3:10)

The people had worked with enthusiasm. (Nehemiah 4:6, TLB)

*The lazy man longs for many things but his hands refuse to work. He is greedy to get, while the godly love to give!
(Proverbs 21:25-26, TLB)*

Do you know a hard-working man? He shall be successful and stand before kings! (Proverbs 22:29)

Hard work brings prosperity; playing around brings poverty. (Proverbs 28:19, TLB)

I even found great pleasure in hard work. (Ecclesiastes 2:10, TLB)

So I saw that there is nothing better for people than to be happy in their work. That is why they are here! (Ecclesiastes 2:10, TLB)

Dreaming instead of doing is foolishness. (Ecclesiastes 5:7, TLB)

WORK

The man who works hard sleeps well whether he eats little or much. (Ecclesiastes 5:12, TLB)

To enjoy your work and to accept your lot in life – that is indeed a gift from God. (Ecclesiastes 5:20, TLB)

Tackle every job that comes along, and if you fear God you can expect his blessing. (Ecclesiastes 7:18, TLB)

If you wait for perfect conditions, you will never get anything done. (Ecclesiastes 11:4, TLB)

Work hard and cheerfully at all you do, just as though you were working for the Lord and not merely for your masters, remembering that it is the Lord Christ who is going to pay you, giving you your full portion of all he owns. He is the one you are really working for. And if you don't do your best for him, he will pay you in a way that you won't like. (Colossians 3:23-25, TLB).

Work hard, like a farmer who gets paid well if he raises a large crop. (2 Timothy 2;6, TLB)

But be you doers. (James 1:22)

Photo courtesy of Chief Stephen Carlisle, Roman Forest Police Department

WORKING WITHOUT RECOGNITION

Photo used with permission

WORKING WITHOUT RECOGNITION

Although not often recognized, dispatchers and other public servants perform critical roles behind the scenes in law enforcement operations.

And some of the parts that seem weakest and least important are really the most necessary. (1 Corinthians 12:23)

We are ignored, even though we are well known. (2 Corinthians 6:9, NLT)

Do nothing from rivalry or conceit, but in humility count others more significant than yourselves. (Philippians 2:3, ESV)

This should be your ambition: to live a quiet life, minding your own business and doing your own work. (1 Thessalonians 4:11, TLB)

God is not unjust; he will not forget your work and the love you have shown him as you have helped his people and continue to help them. (Hebrews 6:10, NIV)

Photo courtesy of Walton County Sheriff Michael Adkinson

Officer John Poulos
Chicago (IL) Police Department

Officer John Poulos

Officer Poulos was off duty, headed home to his neighborhood of Old Town in Chicago. As was his habit, rather than taking the main road, he chose to walk down a darkened alley where a rash of burglaries had plagued the neighborhood. Soon after entering the alley, he noticed an individual on his neighbor's unlit second floor balcony using a flashlight to peer into the darkened residence. Having made it a point to know his neighbors, Officer Poulos knew that the apartment was empty and being renovated. Since Officer Poulos was not in uniform, he identified himself as a police officer and instructed the individual to come down from the balcony.

The individual refused to comply with Officer Poulos' request and began verbally threatening him. Officer Poulos called 911 for assistance and informed dispatch that he was witnessing a burglary in progress. He added that he had confronted the offender, who was both uncooperative and threatening.

Suddenly, the suspect directed the flashlight beam directly into Office Poulos' eyes, momentarily blinding him. Officer Poulos drew his weapon and took cover behind a large dumpster in the alleyway. The suspect descended the staircase all the while keeping his right hand in his waistband—implying that he had a weapon—and repeatedly shouted that he was going to kill Officer Poulos.

OFFICER JOHN POULOS

Realizing that his back-up was still minutes away, Officer Poulos closed the distance between himself and the suspect. As the suspect reached the bottom of the staircase, Officer Poulos instructed the would-be burglar to "show his hands and slowly get on the ground." In response, the suspect lunged at Officer Poulos, attempting to strike him with a metal object that he had pulled from his waistband.

Fearing for his safety and the safety of his neighbors, Officer Poulos fired his weapon twice and took cover until backup arrived on scene. Testimony of eye-witnesses confirmed that Officer Poulos fired his weapon as a last resort, fatally wounding a career criminal who had more than 50 arrests on his record. Discovered in the suspect's possession were several stolen cell phones and jewelry the suspect had obtained from multiple burglaries previously classified as cold cases.

According to Commander Berscott Ruiz of the Chicago Police Department, "Officer Poulos exemplifies all that law enforcement strives to instill in its officers. He could have walked home that night, ignored what he had seen and allowed a career criminal to continue to prey on unsuspecting people. Instead, he acted, and for that, his community, his department and this City are grateful."

REPRINTED WITH PERMISSION FROM THE NATIONAL LAW ENFORCEMENT OFFICERS MEMORIAL FUND.

Photo courtesy of Houston Police Department

Officer Timothy Purdy

Charlotte-Mecklenburg (NC) Police Department

Officer Timothy Purdy

Officer Timothy Purdy was dispatched to be on the lookout for an autistic, and potentially suicidal, teenager who had a long history of violence toward law enforcement officers due to his mental disability. He had left his high school in Charlotte, NC, without permission.

Officer Purdy found the high school student in the parking lot of a local park, and immediately tried to de-escalate the situation when he became aware that the teen was in an agitated state. Trying to connect with the student, Officer Purdy sat next to him in the parking lot and spoke with him for 20 minutes.

As they talked, the young man began to warm up to the officer and laugh, and eventually, was able to get the help that he needed.

"I could tell that it looked like it was going to get into a situation that wasn't going to be good for anybody," Officer Purdy said. "I'm an instructor out at the academy and what I tell officers coming through is 'make sure you treat people the way that you'd want your loved ones to be treated. Picture the situation where that might be your loved one needing help.'"

The officer's interaction with the teenager was documented with a photo posted on the police department's Facebook page, where it gained international recognition.

"Tim (Purdy) doesn't even have Facebook," said Robert Tufano, CMPD PIO. "It's all foreign to him how this whole thing developed."

"The whole situation has been overwhelming from the responses from the community and my fellow officers. I don't think I can say enough what an honor this is. It's surreal at this point, and very humbling," Officer Purdy said.

"Policing goes beyond enforcement," CMPD Chief of Police Kerr Putney said. "Sometimes it's the little things officers do that make the biggest difference."

Reprinted with permission from the National Law Enforcement Officers Memorial Fund.

Photo courtesy of Walton County Sheriff Michael Adkinson

Patrolman Steve Wilson
South Euclid (Ohio) Police Department

Patrolman Steve Wilson

South Euclid Police Department received multiple calls regarding a possible burglary in progress. The responding officers, including Patrolman Wilson, observed signs of forced entry at the back door of the residence, and heard screams for help from a woman inside.

Upon entering the house, the officers announced their presence and followed the screams. Patrolman Wilson entered the living room of the house where he observed a female victim lying on her back with a male suspect kneeling on top of her.

Patrolman Wilson ordered the suspect off the victim. The suspect yelled, "kill me, kill me!" as he raised a large knife and attempted to stab the victim. Patrolman Wilson then fired two shots at the suspect, striking him with both. The shots incapacitated the suspect.

Patrolman Wilson handcuffed the suspect and immediately began treating the victim, who had been stabbed several times prior to the officers' arrival. The suspect was the ex-boyfriend of the victim and had broken into the house to kill her. The suspect later died.

According to Lieutenant James Wilson of the South Euclid Police Department, "there is little doubt that, had Patrolman Wilson not made the decision to use lethal force, the victim would have been murdered by the suspect in her home that morning."

"Patrolman Wilson's quick response to a deadly situation saved the life of the victim," said Memorial Fund Chairman and Chief Executive Officer Craig W. Floyd.

∽

Reprinted with permission from the National Law Enforcement Officers Memorial Fund.

Photo courtesy of Walton County Sheriff Michael Adkinson

Sergeant Adam Johnson
Austin (Texas) Police Department

Sergeant Adam Johnson

In the early morning hours, a lone gunman went on a shooting rampage in downtown Austin. The gunman opened fire, attacking a Mexican consulate and federal courthouse. Officers responded to both locations after receiving 911 calls. It was during this time, that the gunman drove to the headquarters of the Austin Police Department.

As the gunman arrived at headquarters, he exited his vehicle and began firing rounds from a rifle at the building. Meanwhile, Sergeant Johnson and the rest of the Austin Mounted Patrol unit were completing their shift and began unsaddling their horses in the nearby parking garage of the building.

The officers quickly realized that the building was under attack and they moved into position to stop the shooter. When the shooter ceased his gunfire for a brief moment to reload his rifle, Sergeant Johnson used the opportunity to intervene and stop him.

Taking cover behind a pillar in the garage, Sergeant Johnson steadied his aim, as he held the reins of two horses distressed by the commotion, and shot a single bullet at the gunman. Sergeant Johnson struck the gunman from over 100 yards away, killing him instantly and ending the threat. Only the gunman was harmed during the attacks.

SERGEANT ADAM JOHNSON

"For a guy to keep his composure while holding two horses with one hand and taking a one-hand shot with the other hand, it says a lot about the training and professionalism of our police department," stated Austin Police Chief Art Acevedo.

"Sergeant Johnson's quick response to a deadly situation thwarted an attack on his department and perhaps saved the lives of his fellow officers," said Memorial Fund Chairman and Chief Executive Officer Craig W. Floyd.

Reprinted with permission from the National Law Enforcement Officers Memorial Fund.

Photo courtesy of Houston Police Department

Sergeant Jay Cook
New York State Police

Sergeant Jay Cook

Two prisoners escaped from the maximum security Clinton Correctional Facility in Dannemora, New York, about 20 miles south of the Canadian border. The escape initiated a massive weeks-long manhunt with multiple law enforcement agencies involved in the search.

Sergeant Cook was patrolling alone in Constable, New York, when he spotted a man jogging alongside the road. Sergeant Cook exited his patrol car and attempted to speak with the jogger, who proceeded to ignore him and began to flee. Sergeant Cook recognized the man as David Sweat, one of the fugitives who had escaped from the maximum security prison.

The sergeant pursued the fugitive on foot into a field two miles away from the Canadian border when he noticed the suspect running towards a tree line. Concerned that the suspect would escape from his view into the densely forested terrain, Sergeant Cook fired two shots from his weapon, striking the fugitive twice in the torso.

Immediately apprehending the fugitive, Sergeant Cook ended the manhunt that lasted nearly three weeks and involved over 1,300 law enforcement officers. Sweat was serving a life sentence for shooting Deputy Sheriff Kevin Tarsla of the Broome County (NY) Sheriff's Office. Sweat had shot Deputy Sheriff Tarsla 15 times and then ran him over with a vehicle.

Governor Andrew Cuomo of New York said, "Sgt. Cook happened to be from Troop B, which is this area, so he knew the area very well. But he was still alone and it was a very courageous act."

"Sergeant Cook did an excellent job. He realized Sweat was going to make it to a tree line, and possibly could have disappeared—and he fired two shots from his service weapon," New York State Police Superintendent Joseph D'Amico told reporters.

"Sergeant Cook's recognition of the fugitive and his quick response in apprehending the suspect were integral to capturing a cop-killer and securing a community that had been on high alert," said Memorial Fund Chairman and Chief Executive Officer Craig W. Floyd.

Reprinted with permission from the National Law Enforcement Officers Memorial Fund.

Photo courtesy of Houston Police Department

Chief of Police
Jeffery Walters
Philippi (WV) Police Department

Chief of Police Jeffery Walters

A 14-year-old student walked into a classroom at Philip Barbour High School in Philippi, West Virginia, and held 29 students and a teacher hostage at gunpoint.

The teacher maintained order in the classroom and kept the students calm while she convinced the gunman to keep additional students from entering the classroom as class periods were changing. Students attempting to enter the classroom informed school faculty of the situation and they called 911.

Within three minutes of receiving the 911 call, Chief Walters and two other law enforcement officers arrived at the high school. Chief Walters was taken to the classroom where he began communicating with the gunman through the window in the door. After 30 minutes of negotiation, the gunman released all of the hostages.

Over the course of the next two hours, Chief Walters continued to talk with the gunman. After the gunman requested to speak with his pastor, Chief Walters and the pastor convinced the gunman to unload his pistol and surrender.

For years, Chief Walters and the Philippi Police Department have been training for active-shooter barricade situations. Chief Walters became an instructor after working with the San Marcos, Texas-based Advanced Law Enforcement Rapid Response Training (ALERRT) program. This training proved invaluable as Chief Walters took control of this situation, peacefully ending what could have been a tragic incident.

According to Philippi Mayor Charles Mouser, "If it hadn't been for Chief Walters and his training, and his discussion and dialogue with the young guy, as well as the teacher's actions, we would have probably had a big tragedy in that school."

"Chief Walters' quick response to a deadly situation saved the lives of many students and faculty," said Memorial Fund Chairman and Chief Executive Officer Craig W. Floyd.

Reprinted with permission from the National Law Enforcement Officers Memorial Fund.

Photo courtesy of Walton County Sheriff Michael Adkinson

Officer Jessica Hawkins
Greenville (South Carolina) Police Department

Officer Jessica Hawkins

Officer Hawkins participated in a National Alliance on Mental Illness (NAMI) run near downtown Greenville. When the race was over, she was on her way home when she heard a call go out about a female in an electric wheelchair who had fallen down a 20-foot embankment into a creek.

Although off duty and in athletic attire, Officer Hawkins was near the location and was the first officer to arrive at the scene. She observed bystanders watching the woman from the top of the embankment and saw the woman's body submerged under the water, as well as half of her head. Officer Hawkins immediately jumped into action and ran into the creek.

It was clear that the woman had suffered a bad fall, as there was a lot of blood and a serious wound to the back of her head. Officers Hawkins grabbed the woman's head and kept it above water until other responders could arrive on the scene and rescue her from the creek.

Since the incident, Officer Hawkins has visited the woman in the hospital, at the patient's request, so that she could thank the officer for rescuing her. Officer Hawkins also assisted in the process of getting her a new wheelchair.

"Even though saving lives is in every police officer's job description, it is clear that Officer Hawkins has a true calling for policing and went above and beyond the call of duty that day," said Johnathan Bragg, Greenville (SC) Police Department Public Information Officer.

"Officer Hawkins' quick thinking and police training played a large part in saving this woman's life," said Memorial Fund Chairman and Chief Executive Officer Craig W. Floyd.

Reprinted with permission from the National Law Enforcement Officers Memorial Fund.

Photo courtesy of Walton County Sheriff Michael Adkinson

Corporal James L. Cosby Jr.
Division of Capitol Police in the Commonwealth of Virginia

Corporal James L. Cosby Jr.

Corporal Cosby was off duty and driving past a law office when he noticed a man in business attire running from the building. As Corporal Cosby continued to drive, he noticed more people fleeing from an exit. Based on his police training, he concluded an active shooter situation was occurring and turned around to assist.

Corporal Cosby identified himself as an off-duty police officer and was informed by witnesses that an armed man had entered the law office and shot at an attorney before fleeing. As he approached the entrance, he encountered the suspect who was carrying a rifle. Corporal Cosby identified himself as a police officer, drew his weapon, and ordered the suspect to drop his rifle.

The suspect repeatedly asked Corporal Cosby to shoot and kill him. As the suspect continued to disobey demands to put his weapon down, Corporal Cosby began engaging the man in conversation as he closed the distance between them. He grabbed the suspect as a responding officer arrived at the scene and assisted him with disarming and subduing the suspect.

The attorney who had been targeted and a bystander were slightly injured during the incident. The suspect had been upset with the attorney for his involvement in a child custody case. The suspect was convicted on five charges, including attempted murder, abduction, unlawfully shooting into an occupied dwelling and two counts of felonious use of a firearm.

According to Colonel Anthony Pike, "As a result of his selfless act of bravery, Corporal Cosby was able to end the rampage of an active shooter incident while also avoiding a potential 'suicide by cop' scenario."

※

REPRINTED WITH PERMISSION FROM THE NATIONAL LAW ENFORCEMENT OFFICERS MEMORIAL FUND.

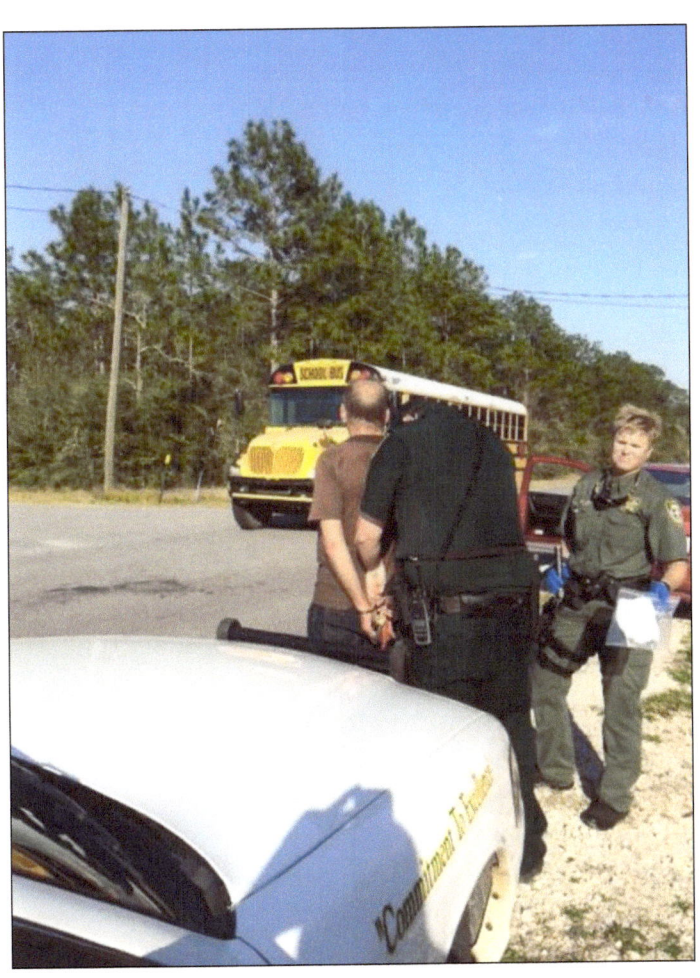

Photo courtesy of Walton County Sheriff Michael Adkinson

Sergeant Anthony Schnacky and Officer Matthew Curry
Rosenberg (TX) Police Department

Sergeant Anthony Schnacky and Officer Matthew Curry

Rosenberg police officers were dispatched to a serious, single-vehicle crash. Upon arriving at the scene, Sergeant Schnacky located a pickup truck overturned on its side.

Sergeant Schnacky accessed the scene and was able to make contact with the driver through the shattered back window. The driver informed Sergeant Schnacky that his leg was broken and that he was trapped inside the vehicle as it quickly began to fill with smoke.

Officer Curry arrived at the scene and rushed to assist Sergeant Schnacky. The two officers quickly determined that they must extract the driver regardless of his injuries as the heat and flames rapidly grew. Risking their lives, Sergeant Schnacky and Officer Curry pulled the driver from the burning vehicle to safety. Within two minutes the truck was completely engulfed in flames. Sergeant Schnacky and Officer Curry's heroic rescue was caught on film by a dashboard camera.

According to Rosenberg (TX) Police Department Patrol Lieutenant Cody Dailey, "Without their commitment, in the fear of danger, the driver of this vehicle might not have survived." The driver of the vehicle suffered a broken leg and shoulder.

"Sergeant Schnacky and Officer Curry's quick thinking and heroic actions enabled them to save this citizen from the burning truck," said Memorial Fund Chairman and Chief Executive Officer Craig W. Floyd.

∽

REPRINTED WITH PERMISSION FROM THE NATIONAL LAW ENFORCEMENT OFFICERS MEMORIAL FUND.

Photo courtesy of Walton County Sheriff Michael Adkinson

Officer James Cunningham
San Francisco (CA) Police Department-Airport Bureau

Officer James Cunningham

Officer James Cunningham was on patrol at the San Francisco International Airport when he heard a Code 33 over the radio, indicating a plane was down. Asiana Airlines Flight 214 carrying 307 passengers clipped a rocky seawall while attempting to land, causing fire and smoke to erupt from the plane as jet fuel poured onto the runway.

Officer Cunningham immediately headed to the scene of the crash, directing a passing ambulance to follow him to assist with the rescue.

When he arrived at the scene, Officer Cunningham began assisting those in need. Officer Cunningham worked with the airplane's crew to rescue the passengers, providing the crew with his knife to cut passengers free from their seats as he carried or directed them to safety.

Just as crew members believed they had cleared the plane of all the passengers, Officer Cunningham realized that the tail of the plane had been torn off in the crash and passengers were still trapped in that section of the plane. The seats of the airplane had been ripped from the floorboards; luggage and debris covered the remaining passengers making it difficult for rescue workers to reach them.

Without regard for his own safety, Officer Cunningham ran into the burning tail of the plane without any protective gear. He cleared a path for rescue workers to reach the remaining passengers and began carrying passengers to safety, not stopping until the last passenger was removed.

According to his former commanding officer Albert Pardini, "Officer Cunningham was in the midst of a disaster and immediately went into action. He had sufficient time to assess the situation and make the decision to approach the aircraft—which could have easily exploded into a ball of fire—so he could rescue the passengers and crew."

"Officer Cunningham relied on his training and immediately sprang into action to save lives," said Memorial Fund Chairman and Chief Executive Officer Craig W. Floyd. "Without regard for his safety, Officer Cunningham ran toward danger to rescue stranded passengers from a burning airplane.

Reprinted with permission from the National Law Enforcement Officers Memorial Fund.

Photo courtesy of Walton County Sheriff Michael Adkinson

Sergeant Philip B. Gingerella, Sr.
Charlestown (RI) Police Department

Sergeant Philip B. Gingerella, Sr.

The Charlestown Emergency Dispatch Center received a frantic 911 call reporting a distressed boogie boarder trapped in a strong riptide current and unable to return to shore at the Blue Shutters Town Beach in Rhode Island. Due to heavy rainfall, the beach was closed, and no lifeguards were on duty to help the man in need.

Sergeant Philip Gingerella and fellow emergency responders arrived at the scene, spotting the man over 300 feet away from the shoreline. Two rescue vessels were dispatched to assist but were delayed due to the dangerous and rough water conditions. With the man growing weaker by the minute and no rescue vessels in sight, emergency responders put a plan into motion. Applying his over 20 years of experience as a lifeguard, Sergeant Gingerella determined that he could execute the water rescue.

Sergeant Gingerella quickly removed his uniform, body armor, gun belt and boots. He put on a life jacket and attached himself to a reel rope. With the aid of a floatation device, Sergeant Gingerella swam against the large breaking waves and rip current to reach the stranded victim. Sergeant Gingerella gave the man the floatation device and attached him to the safety rope. Together, the two made it to safety with the assistance of the rescuers on shore.

SERGEANT PHILIP B. GINGERELLA, SR.

According to Charlestown Chief of Police Jeffrey Allen, "Sergeant Philip Gingerella demonstrated great bravery and went above and beyond the call of duty. He took the initiative to attempt the surf rescue himself. Sergeant Gingerella, knowing he possessed the knowledge and ability to perform the water rescue, put his knowledge and training to use."

Reprinted with permission from the National Law Enforcement Officers Memorial Fund.

Photo courtesy of Walton County Sheriff Michael Adkinson

Trooper First Class Joshua Kim
Maryland State Police

Trooper Joshua Kim

Trooper Kim was patrolling the Millard E. Tydings Memorial Bridge, 90 feet above the Susquehanna River on I-95 in Harford County, Maryland, when he noticed something was amiss. He spotted a man walking along the side of the busy bridge away from a nearby parked car. Trooper Kim immediately made a U-turn and went back to check on the man.

As soon as Trooper Kim pulled up behind the man, he turned and waved at Trooper Kim, and then began climbing over the three foot barrier to jump off the bridge. With no regard for his own safety, Trooper Kim darted from his vehicle and grabbed the man around his waist to prevent him from climbing over the concrete barrier. Relying on his past experience as a football player, Trooper Kim lowered his body as he grabbed the man so that he would not be pulled over the barricade with him. Trooper Kim handcuffed the man to prevent him from harming himself by running into traffic, before taking him to an area hospital for evaluation. Trooper Kim's heroic rescue was caught on film by his vehicle's dashboard camera.

Trooper Kim has been a Maryland State Trooper for approximately two and a half years and is assigned to the JFK Memorial Highway Barracks in Perryville, Maryland.

"Trooper First Class Kim's bravery, selflessness and dedication to public safety are what make him truly one of 'Maryland's Finest' and an example to all law enforcement," shared Lieutenant Ronald Diggs, Executive Officer, MSP Field Operations Bureau.

"Trooper Kim's decisive intervention saved the life of this citizen," said Memorial Fund Chairman & CEO Craig Floyd.

Reprinted with permission from the National Law Enforcement Officers Memorial Fund.

Photo courtesy of Walton County Sheriff Michael Adkinson

Officer Nicholas Simons
United States Capitol Police

Officer Nicholas Simons

Officer Simons was on assignment in the Hart Senate Office Building in Washington, DC when he was alerted by a bystander that a man had collapsed outside of the Constitution Avenue entrance, possibly having a heart attack. Officer Simons immediately sprang to action by first putting out a "priority" call for the medical emergency, as well as requesting DC Fire Department (DCFD) assistance and an Automatic External Defibrillator (AED).

When Officer Simons reached the man, he noted the gentleman was unconscious, not breathing, and turning blue. Officer Simons immediately began applying life-saving techniques, including chest compressions and rescue breaths, until the AED arrived. After Officer Simons applied the AED to the man, it indicated that a shock was needed and Officer Simons delivered one shock to the individual.

Once the shock was delivered, Officer Simons continued applying chest compressions, which ultimately led to the individual regaining consciousness. The man was breathing by the time DCFD arrived on the scene. Rescue personnel transported the man and a member of his group to the hospital, where he was met by his wife.

Later that afternoon, the spouse called the U.S. Capitol Police to give an update on her husband. First, she expressed her deepest gratitude to the U.S. Capitol Police and especially to Officer Simons for saving her husband's life. She indicated that the doctors were baffled as to why her husband's heart just stopped, but that he was alive today because trained police officers reacted quickly.

"I am extremely proud of our officers who responded swiftly to render aid during this medical emergency," said U.S. Capitol Police Chief Kim Dine. "This was a true team effort, and Officer Simons is commended for his quick and heroic actions in saving another man's life."

"Officer Simon's quick actions, police training, and instincts enabled him to save the life of this citizen," said Memorial Fund Chairman & CEO Craig Floyd.

Reprinted with permission from the National Law Enforcement Officers Memorial Fund.

Photo courtesy of Walton County Sheriff Michael Adkinson

Deputy U. S. Marshals (DUSMs) Matthew Barger, Michael Cifu, Andrew Kottke, and Frank Morales
United States Marshals Service

Left to right: Deputy U. S. Marshals Frank Morales, Andrew Kottke, Michael Cifu and Matthew Barger

Ms. Valerie Tillet, a District of Columbia Court employee, was returning from her lunch break when she was struck by a dump truck while traversing a crosswalk. Witnesses at the scene watched in horror as the dump truck then began to backup, pinning her and crushing her legs.

Deputy U.S. Marshalls (DUSM's) Matthew Barger and Michael Cifu were returning to the Moultrie Courthouse from their lunch break when they came upon the scene. The two immediately ran to Ms. Tillet, who had suffered severe injuries to her lower extremities and was losing blood profusely. Deputy U.S. Marshalls Barger and Cifu assessed the situation and utilized their training and experience to render first aid, including the use of an improvised tourniquet to try and stop her massive blood loss.

DEPUTY U.S. MARSHALS (DUSMS) MATTHEW BARGER, MICHAEL CIFU, ANDREW KOTTKE, AND FRANK MORALES

Deputy U.S. Marshalls Andrew Kottke and Frank Morales arrived on the scene soon after the incident. Surveying the chaos of the scene and the growing number of on-lookers, Deputy U.S. Marshalls Kottke and Morales took control of the scene and began relaying information to emergency medical and law enforcement personnel.

Upon their arrival, District of Columbia Fire and Emergency Medical Services (DC Fire/EMS) personnel praised the life-saving work of Deputy U.S. Marshalls Barger and Cifu. The responding medics stated that if the care rendered by Deputy U.S. Marshalls Barger and Cifu had not been provided, Ms. Tillet would have had a drastically reduced chance of survival. The supporting roles of Deputy U.S. Marshalls Kottke and Morales were instrumental in maintaining the safety of all parties involved. Without the efforts of DUSMs Kottke and Morales, it would have been impossible for DUSMs Barger and Cifu to focus on providing first aid.

"When I think about that day, I never saw their faces but I could hear their voices. I want to say thank you to these fine gentlemen for the work they did ... they answered the call. They could have kept going, but they didn't. So I want to say thank you, thank you, thank you. God bless you," Ms. Tillet shared.

"The U. S. Marshals Service commends deputy marshals Barger, Cifu, Kottke and Morales on their vigilance, demeanor, situational awareness and execution of critical care in this tragic incident," said Supervisory Deputy United States Marshal Aaron Sawyer. "These deputy marshals' outstanding performance exemplifies the standards and expectations of the U. S. Marshals Service."

Reprinted with permission from the National Law Enforcement Officers Memorial Fund.

Chief of Police Thomas Fowler, Sergeant Robert Roy, Officer Michael Alder, and Officer Justin Murphy

Salisbury (MA) Police Department and Seabrook (NH) Police Department

Left to right: Chief Thomas Fowler, Officer Michael Alder, Sergeant Robert Roy and Officer Justin Murphy

The Salisbury (MA) Police Department received a 911 call indicating that police and ambulances were needed at a location where a man and woman had been brutally attacked and stabbed in what was believed to be a domestic dispute.

Sergeant Roy was one of the first officers to respond to the scene. As he arrived, the suspect attempted to flee by aiming his car directly at Sergeant Roy's cruiser. Sergeant Roy was forced to abruptly turn the wheel of his police car to avoid a head-on collision. This action caused the suspect to strike a second responding officer's car, belonging to Officer Alder. Although Officer Alder's airbags deployed during the collision, he was able to extricate himself from the passenger side of his vehicle.

The suspect was observed wielding both a machete and a knife, which he then used to threaten the responding officers. The suspect stated that he wanted the responding officers to shoot him. Officer Alder attempted to engage the suspect in conversation and convince him to put down his weapons, but the suspect remained agitated and threatening.

CHIEF OF POLICE THOMAS FOWLER, SERGEANT ROBERT ROY, OFFICER MICHAEL ALDER, AND OFFICER JUSTIN MURPHY

Salisbury Police Chief Fowler overheard dispatches related to the incident and arrived on the scene, immediately retrieving an AR-15 patrol rifle from the trunk of his vehicle. Officer Justin Murphy soon arrived on scene and suddenly, the suspect's demeanor escalated and he became more aggressive.

The suspect began advancing on the officers. Chief Fowler directed Officer Murphy to deploy his Taser on the suspect, but it had little effect on slowing or stopping his advancement toward the officers. Chief Fowler and Officer Alder were forced to use their weapons on the suspect, each firing two shots. The suspect was pronounced dead at the scene. The stabbing victims went on to recover from their attack.

"These officers continue to protect and serve their respective communities," said Bryan McMahon, Executive Secretary of the New England Police Benevolent Association. "Their selfless acts and distinguished service should not go unacknowledged. They are true and fine representatives of the law enforcement community."

"These four officers deserve to be recognized for their gallantry in the face of obvious danger," said Lieutenant and Executive Officer Anthony King of the Salisbury (MA) Police Department. "They responded without fear or hesitation in order to assist the victims, the residents of Salisbury who live in the immediate area, and each other. Despite being faced with this armed and obviously violent subject, these officers made every attempt to end this standoff in a peaceful manner, while always knowingly placing themselves in between the suspect and the public," he continued. "This incident is the most impressive display of teamwork and professionalism that I have ever experienced in my twenty-three years as a police officer."

"These officer's quick actions and police instincts enabled them to save their community from further danger," said Memorial Fund Chairman & CEO Craig Floyd.

Reprinted with permission from the National Law Enforcement Officers Memorial Fund.

Officer Christopher Nebbeling
West Palm Beach (FL) Police Department

Officer Christopher Nebbeling
West Palm Beach (FL) Police Department

West Palm Beach officers were pursuing suspects of a reported shooting. The West Palm Beach Police Department issued an alert on the suspect's vehicle, stating they were last seen in a dark sports utility vehicle heading south towards a crowded downtown area.

Officer Nebbeling was monitoring a Halloween event nearby, when he heard gunshots. As Officer Nebbeling headed towards the scene to assist, he noticed an SUV matching the description of the suspect's vehicle traveling in the opposite direction at a high speed, and he pursued the vehicle. The SUV accelerated and weaved between cars through heavy traffic to elude Officer Nebbeling. The SUV entered a major intersection and nearly struck several motorists before the driver lost control of the vehicle, eventually crashing into the median. The driver stopped the SUV, and the suspects fled on foot.

As Officer Nebbeling exited his squad car to pursue the suspects, he saw a rear passenger exit the SUV carrying an assault rifle. The suspect aimed his weapon at Officer Nebbeling. An eight-year Army veteran who served in Iraq and Afghanistan, Officer Nebbeling instinctively drew his service weapon and advanced towards the threat, firing until the gun-wielding suspect was disabled. Officer Nebbeling restrained him until reinforcements could arrive and then remained at the scene to render aid.

Police later captured the other two suspects. The suspect with the assault rifle succumbed to his injuries later that evening. He was a gang member with a long arrest record, including involvement in three shootings in prior years. One of those shootings was just a few weeks before the incident. The suspect's weapon was discovered to be a loaded AK-47.

"When thrust into this situation, Officer Nebbeling acted heroically," said Sergeant Adam Myers of the West Palm Beach (FL) Police Department. "In the face of superior firepower, Officer Nebbeling stared directly at the threat, advanced and eliminated it. If it weren't for the decision-making and actions of Officer Nebbeling, unknown numbers of police and civilians could have suffered serious bodily harm, if not death."

"Officer Nebbeling's quick actions and police instincts enabled him to save his community from further danger," said Memorial Fund Chairman & CEO Craig Floyd.

Reprinted with permission from the National Law Enforcement Officers Memorial Fund.

Photo courtesy of Houston Police Department

Lieutenant Jerald Wheeler
Southaven (MS) Police Department

Lieutenant Jerald Wheeler
Southaven (MS) Police Department

Lieutenant Wheeler believed that a memorial needed to be built in his community to honor the fallen officers of DeSoto County. The National Law Enforcement Officers Memorial is more than a thousand miles from DeSoto County, and the families and friends of fallen officers would need to travel a long way to visit this peaceful place devoted to their loved ones. Lieutenant Wheeler's close friend and fellow officer, Lieutenant James William Vance, Jr, was shot and killed in the line of duty on October 7, 1988, a loss that heavily influenced Lieutenant Wheeler's decision to build a memorial in his community.

Lieutenant Wheeler and other community members founded the DeSoto County Public Safety committee. Together, they raised nearly $100,000 in donations and in December 2004, the DeSoto Public Safety Officer Memorial was officially dedicated. The memorial is located at the DeSoto County Courthouse in Hernando, MS. A special remembrance ceremony is held at the memorial on the first Friday of May each year.

Following the dedication of the memorial, the DeSoto County Public Safety Committee still had funds remaining. Lieutenant Wheeler led the effort to use the extra money to establish a scholarship fund with Northwest Mississippi Community College. The committee created eight named endowments to honor each of the fallen officers from DeSoto County. Scholarships have been awarded to students majoring in public service areas like Criminal Justice, EMT-Paramedic, and Nursing.

Throughout his 30-year career in law enforcement, Lieutenant Wheeler has worked on various programs within his community. He is responsible for creating the Southaven Police Department's Volunteer in Policing program and Citizen's Police Academy and is also a co-founder of the Southaven Police Department's Explorers Program. Lieutenant Wheeler is also in charge of the department's School Resource Officer division and visits as many as five local schools each day.

"We are so very proud of Lt. Wheeler and the excellent work he always does for our department and community." said Tom Long, Chief of the Southaven (MS) Police Department.

Reprinted with permission from the National Law Enforcement Officers Memorial Fund.

Photo courtesy of Houston Police Department

Trooper Brian Beuning
Minnesota State Patrol

Trooper Brian Beuning

Trooper Beuning responded to a 911 call from a woman who was trapped in a car that was stranded in floodwaters near Beaver Creek, MN. The area had experienced heavy rains, causing wide-spread flooding throughout the northern and southern parts of the state. The woman was driving through a flooded area of I-90 when she lost control of her car and drifted towards a water-filled ditch. The water rose quickly around her vehicle and began to seep into its interior. The woman called 911, realizing how much danger she was in.

Once he arrived at the scene, Trooper Beuning immediately waded out into the knee-deep water to the woman's car, ignoring the risk that he could be swept away by the rising floodwaters at any moment. Once he reached the car, Trooper Beuning calmly instructed the woman to pull the car's emergency break and crawl into the back seat so she could escape through the rear window. Once the woman complied, Trooper Beuning quickly pulled the woman out of the car.

Just seconds after the woman escaped, the car was swept away by the flood waters and sank down into the ditch before drifting away into the flooded field beyond.

Because the floodwaters' were too strong for the two to escape without assistance, Trooper Beuning held on to the woman and braced himself against the flood's strong currents until help could arrive. As time dragged on, the woman began to lose hope, fearing that she would perish and that her young daughter would have to grow up without a mother. Trooper Beuning, a father himself, continuously assured the woman that they would be rescued, saying repeatedly "We're going to do this for our kids."

Because the floodwaters were too swift and strong, a boat launched by the Department of Natural Resources was unable to reach Trooper Beuning and the woman. Two firefighters in water rescue suits were sent in to rescue the stranded pair. The firefighters placed life jackets on both Trooper Beuning and woman, securing them with a rope attached to a semi-truck. Forty-five minutes after becoming trapped in the floodwaters, Trooper Beuning and the women were back safely on dry land.

The woman credits Trooper Beuning with saving her life, saying, "If it wasn't for him [Trooper Beuning], I wouldn't be here today."

"The Minnesota State Patrol is proud of Trooper Brian Beuning receiving this award. The courage he displayed on June 16th undoubtedly saved Julisa Jones from harm," said Lt. Colonel Matt Langer, Acting Chief of the MN State Patrol. "Trooper Beuning did not hesitate to risk his own safety to help someone else, demonstrating the commitment to public safety by members of the Minnesota State Patrol and peace officers everywhere."

Reprinted with permission from the National Law Enforcement Officers Memorial Fund.

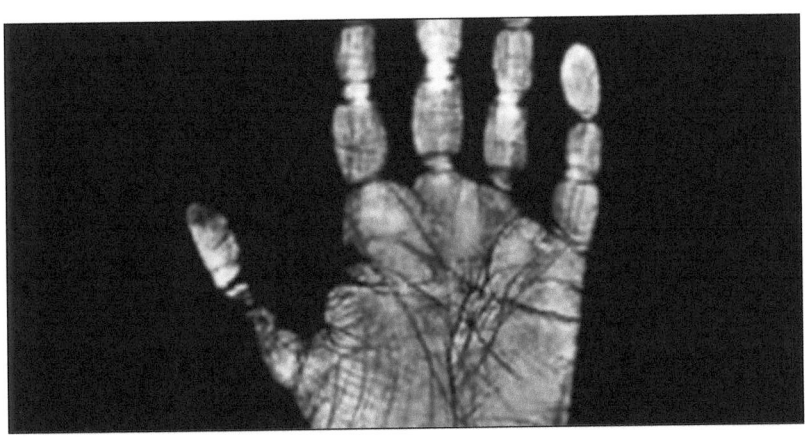

Photo courtesy of Houston Police Department

Senior Investigator John Vescio
New York State Police

Senior Investigator John Vescio

Investigator Vescio was off-duty when he stopped at a busy gas station to fill up his department vehicle. He was standing at the pump next to his vehicle when suddenly a sedan slammed into the opposite side of the pump. The sedan struck the pump with such force that it hit Investigator Vescio and immediately caught on fire.

Following his instincts, Investigator Vescio quickly ran away from the burning pump and vehicles. However, once he reached a safe distance, he realized that there was an elderly man slumped over in the sedan, which was rapidly being consumed by fire. Disregarding his own safety, Investigator Vescio ran back toward the burning car in order to save the elderly man.

Investigator Vescio reached the sedan and discovered the elderly man was unresponsive and pinned inside the vehicle due to the damage caused by the impact. Investigator Vescio unfastened the man's seatbelt and tried to pull him out of the car. After several attempts, he was able to get the man free of the car and drag him to safety.

After removing the victim from his damaged vehicle, Investigator Vescio again placed himself in danger by returning to the fire in order to retrieve his first aid kit from the trunk of his vehicle. With the kit, Investigator Vescio was able to perform first aid on the elderly man until medical personnel arrived on the scene. Miraculously, Investigator Vescio and the crash victim escaped from the incident with no injuries. Later, it was revealed that the elderly man had suffered from a diabetic episode and passed out, causing him to lose control of his vehicle and crash into the pump.

Regarding the incident, Major Keith Corlett of the New York State Police Department said, "I think John [Investigator Vescio] did a very heroic thing. He starts off as a civilian, becomes a victim, and then his police training kicks in and he actually saved somebody's life."

Reprinted with permission from the National Law Enforcement Officers Memorial Fund.

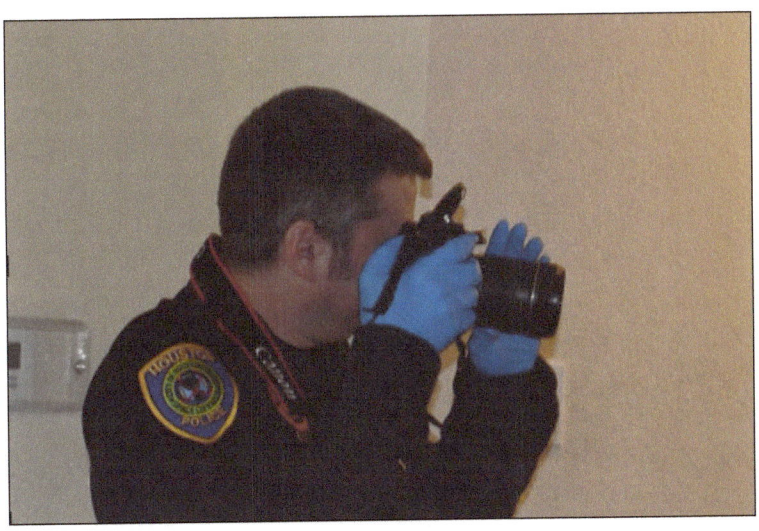

Photo courtesy of Houston Police Department

Deputy Brian Matthews
Van Buren County (MI) Sheriff's Office

Deputy Brian Matthews

After completing a week's training in Arizona, 19 newly certified Drug Recognition Expert (DRE) trained officers and instructors were on a flight back to Michigan. An hour after takeoff, a flight attendant called for a medically trained passenger to assist another passenger in need. DRE Deputy Brian Matthews offered to help.

Deputy Matthews recognized the passenger in distress as a fellow officer, Muskegon (MI) Police Officer John Burns, who had just completed the DRE training as well. Deputy Matthews stabilized Officer Burns using the limited equipment he had on hand and assessed that Officer Burns was suffering a stroke. Realizing that his condition was worsening, Deputy Matthews informed the flight attendant that Officer Burns needed immediate medical attention and advised that the aircraft should make an emergency landing.

The pilot safely landed the plane in Des Moines, Iowa. Deputy Matthews stayed with Officer Burns, improvised an oxygen mask from an overhead compartment mask and kept Officer Burns as comfortable as possible during the landing. Deputy Matthews directed another fellow officer to take notes of his assessment to give emergency medical personnel on the ground.

Officer Burns, who was unconscious at this time, was immediately transported to a Level 1 Trauma/Stroke facility in downtown Des Moines. With the information provided by the notes of the assessment, hospital personnel estimated that 83 minutes had passed from the time the symptoms began to the time medical personnel administered the medicine, Tissue Plasminogen Activator (t-PA), which is most effective when administered within three hours of the onset of symptoms in order to reduce the impact of the stroke. If Deputy Matthews had not taken the quick action in requesting an emergency landing, the plane's next stop would have been Chicago, which would have likely been too late for the medicine to work effectively. Two days after the incident, Officer Burns was walking with assistance, though he still showed signs of the stroke.

Reprinted with permission from the National Law Enforcement Officers Memorial Fund.

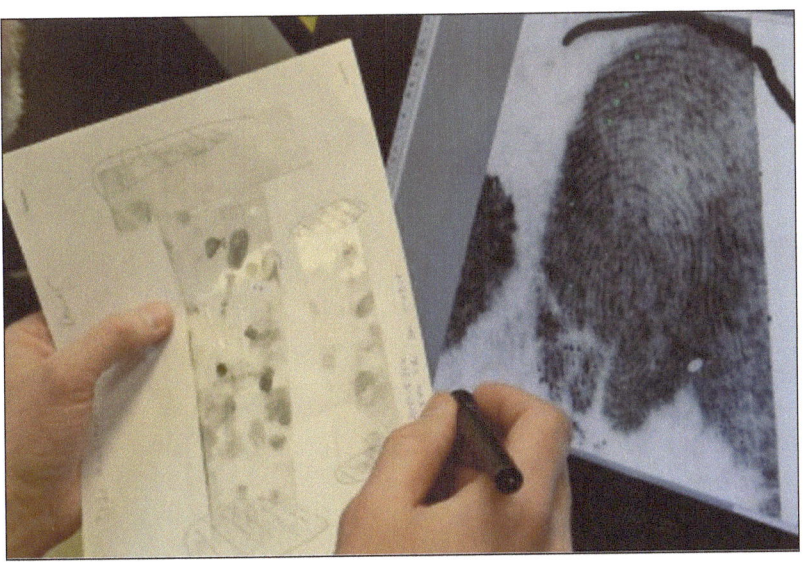

Photo courtesy of Houston Police Department

Officer Matthew Bowling and Officer Vincent Martucci
U.S. Customs and Border Protection

Customs and Border Protection Officers Matthew Bowling and Vincent Martucci

Hurricane Sandy made landfall in New York City. A full moon generated unusually high tides and amplified Sandy's storm surge. Ocean water gushed over seawalls, streets flooded, and trees and power lines were knocked down. Emergency call centers were overloaded and few calls got through. After several unsuccessful attempts to reach a 911 operator, Customs and Border Patrol (CBP) Officer Mariano Fontana placed a frantic call to the CBP Command Center at John F. Kennedy International Airport. He explained that he and his family were trapped in the attic of their home, located just blocks from the ocean, in Howard Beach, Queens. At the time of the call, the lower levels of the residence were already completely flooded.

Customs and Border Patrol Officers Matthew Bowling and Vincent Martucci, along with CBP Chief David Bello, responded to the call. Due to the extreme weather conditions, it took more than 30 minutes for the officers to drive the six miles to the Fontana's home. With winds exceeding 75 mph, along with the pounding rain, the flooding and debris covering the roadways, the closest the officers could get to the house was four city blocks away. Officers Bowling and Martucci parked their vehicle, grabbed over 50 pounds of equipment, and ventured into the neck deep water.

Downed electrical lines and debris hampered their progress. At times they had to swim, rather than walk, as the flood levels exceeded six feet. During this dangerous trek, the officers took turns motivating one another to keep going. When they located the residence, they were relieved to learn that the family was safe. The next task was to determine the safest way to evacuate the family from the residence. Officers Bowling and Martucci stayed in constant contact with the CBP Command Center, and soon a secure evacuation route was established. However, Officers Bowling and Martucci realized that other residents on that street might need assistance as well. The two officers went door-to-door to the neighboring homes to offer their help before escorting the Fontana family to the Customs and Border Patrol personnel waiting to transport them to a safe location.

More than 280 people lost their lives as Superstorm Sandy wreaked havoc from the Caribbean islands, up the East coast to Canada, and out to the Appalachians and the Midwest. If not for the bravery of Officers Bowling and Martucci, the Fontana family might have been included in that staggering statistic.

According to Customs and Border Protection Officer Monyr Thabet, "Officers Bowling and Martucci rose above and beyond the call of duty when faced with imminent danger to help those in need."

Reprinted with permission from the National Law Enforcement Officers Memorial Fund.

Lieutenant Timothy Jungel
Eaton County, Michigan Sheriff's Office

Lieutenant Timothy Jungel

The loss of a law enforcement officer in the line of duty is felt by many—family and friends, colleagues, the department, and the community as a whole. Lieutenant Timothy Jungel recognized the important fact that when the unthinkable happens and an officer dies on the job, those devastated by the death often require assistance to deal with the tragedy.

To assist the family, friends, and colleagues of fallen officers, Lieutenant Jungel was instrumental in creating the Michigan Sheriff's & Municipal Memorial Assistance Response Team (S.M.M.A.R.T.). Since 2003, this team has responded immediately to line of duty deaths throughout the state of Michigan. The team's purpose is to help the family and department by alleviating the stress of planning a funeral in order to allow them to take time for themselves to begin healing and dealing with other emergencies. The team is available 24-hours a day, responds to the community following the tragedy, and remains on-site until the final call. There is no cost to the requesting agency for S.M.M.A.R.T.'s services.

An important element of a law enforcement memorial service is the role of the Honor Guard unit, which traditionally helps plan the ceremonial aspects and logistics of the service. As the Honor Guard/Color Guard Coordinator for his agency, Lieutenant Jungel is responsible for the "casket watch," the visitation, and the funeral and graveside services. He also coordinates the pallbearers, the bagpiper, and the bugler. Lieutenant Jungel has attended every funeral the Michigan Sheriff's Association's S.M.M.A.R.T. team has assisted with since its inception in 2003.

In addition to this tremendous effort in Michigan, Lieutenant Jungel travels across the country to both national and statewide conferences to present information about the S.M.M.A.R.T. team to other agencies. Should another agency wish to develop its own program, he is there to assist in any way possible. Lieutenant Jungel also administers an Honor Guard and Color Guard training school which is attended by law enforcement officers and firefighters from across Michigan and neighboring states. The team has been extremely successful and has recently expanded to include the Michigan Association of Chiefs of Police as a joint partner. Lieutenant Jungel has volunteered hundreds of off-duty hours to service the needs of his professional family. He sets a high standard for those in law enforcement of leadership by example.

Lieutenant Timothy Jungel has served with the Eaton County (MI) Sheriff's Office for 19 years. In addition to his current duties as a Lieutenant and as the department's Honor Guard Coordinator, he also serves the department as a firearms instructor and is a member of the Special Response Team (SRT).

Reprinted with permission from the National Law Enforcement Officers Memorial Fund.

Photo courtesy of Walton County Sheriff Michael Adkinson

Deputy Sheriff Jeffrey Brunkow
Boulder County (CO) Sheriff's Office

Deputy Sheriff Jeffrey Brunkow

Deputy Brunkow and fellow deputies from the Boulder County Sheriff's Office responded to a situation in which a man was holding two of his in-laws hostage at gunpoint. The suspect had taken his father-in-law and brother-in-law hostage after his estranged wife left him.

Deputies located the suspect and the hostages inside a car in a parking lot, where the suspect was pointing a gun at the hostages and threatening to kill them. The suspect opened a rear door of the vehicle and waved the gun at the officers, warning them to stay back.

The suspect pulled the weapon back into the vehicle, leaving the door slightly open. The car windows had dark tinting, making it impossible to see inside the car. Through the small opening of the door, Deputy Brunkow saw the suspect put the gun to the back of a hostage's head.

Fearing for the life of the hostage, Deputy Brunkow fired a single shot from roughly 120 feet away through the 4-inch car door opening, striking the suspect in the head and killing him instantly.

The victims scrambled from the car and ran to the deputies. They later told the deputies, "You saved our lives."

"That shot had saved their lives," Boulder County Sheriff Joe Pelle said. "The suspect had just told his brother-in-law to open his eyes and look to the mountains because 'it's the last thing you're ever gonna see'."

The suspect had battered his estranged wife and made threats to kill her and her family for several months leading up to the hostage situation.

"There is no doubt that Deputy Brunkow's courageous act saved the lives of the hostages," said Memorial Fund Chairman and Chief Executive Officer Craig W. Floyd.

Reprinted with permission from the National Law Enforcement Officers Memorial Fund.

Photo courtesy of Walton County Sheriff Michael Adkinson

Officer Sean O'Brien
Evanston (IL) Police Department

Officer Sean O'Brien

Officer Sean O'Brien was spending his day off running errands with his girlfriend. As they headed home in the midst of a snowstorm, they observed a young boy in the middle of a busy intersection. Out of concern for the boy's safety, and due to the increasingly dangerous weather conditions that day, Officer O'Brien pulled his vehicle off to the shoulder of the road and set out to speak to the child.

The young autistic boy had slipped away from his grandmother and was enamored by the Des Planes River. Officer O'Brien then saw the child pick up a large chunk of snow, hurl it into the freezing water below him, and jump into the river after it. Without hesitation, Officer O'Brien followed the boy into the frigid, waist-deep river. Though he could not see the boy, Officer O'Brien faintly noticed the orange Chicago Bears hat the boy was wearing. As quickly as he could, Officer O'Brien pulled the boy out of the river and brought him back to his vehicle. He turned the car heater up as high as it would go in an attempt to maintain the child's body temperature and called emergency services. Shortly after, the child was taken to a local hospital for medical treatment and released later that day.

Once the boy's parents were located, they explained that their son had wandered off from his grandmother's house to play in the snow.

According to Commander Angela Hearts-Glass of the Evanston (IL) Police Department, "The temperature of the water was near freezing and the current could have swept the child away. Officer O'Brien acted without concern for his own safety. It is without dispute that Officer O'Brien performed a true act of heroism and bravery."

This admiration for Officer O'Brien is echoed by Commander Joseph Dugan. "Officer O'Brien is a hard-working police officer who has the ability to be proactive in making arrests while still maintaining a positive relationship with members of the community where he patrols."

Reprinted with permission from the National Law Enforcement Officers Memorial Fund.

Photo courtesy of Walton County Sheriff Michael Adkinson

Trooper Rick Carlson | Trooper Jim Leonard
Deputy Justin Holzschu
Michigan State Police | Otsego County (MI) Sheriff's Department

Left to right: Trooper Rick Carlson and Trooper Jim Leonard of the Michigan State Police, and Deputy Justin Holzschu of the Otsego County (MI) Sheriff's Department

A babysitter near Gaylord, MI, awoke to find the house in which she was watching two children on fire. The babysitter was able to get a seven-year-old girl out of the house, but the flames kept her from reaching two-year-old Kingston, who was sleeping in a bedroom in the back of the home. She ran to a neighbor's house to call 911.

Troopers Jim Leonard and Rick Carlson received the call from dispatch and were on the scene within five minutes, followed closely by Deputy Justin Holzschu. The troopers and deputy tried to make their way into the house, but the fire and smoke made it impossible. Upon learning that a child was in the back of the house, the officers broke through glass patio doors, but were unsuccessful in making it more than a few feet before being overcome by smoke.

Deputy Holzschu then broke windows on the side of the house to let smoke escape, allowing Troopers Leonard and Carlson to enter the house and rescue the unresponsive child from his crib.

Immediately exiting the house, the troopers began performing CPR on the boy and were able to restore breathing and a pulse. Both children were taken to the hospital, where they recovered.

"We're humbled by their bravery, by their response and for risking their lives," said Lt. Derrick Carroll, Assistant Post Commander of the Michigan State Police Gaylord Post. "They saved that baby."

"If they didn't get there and do what they did, the child may have died," said Otsego County Undersheriff Matt Muladore.

"The actions of these three heroes saved the life of a small child," Memorial Fund Chairman and CEO Craig W. Floyd said. "They never gave up, repeatedly putting their lives in danger.

Reprinted with permission from the National Law Enforcement Officers Memorial Fund.

Photo courtesy of Walton County Sheriff Michael Adkinson

Sergeant John Conneely and Officer Michael Modzelewski
Chicago (IL) Police Department

Sergeant John Conneely (left) and Officer Michael Modzelewski

Shots rang out in the violence-plagued South Side of Chicago. Officer Michael Modzelewski and then-Officer John Conneely responded to a drive-by shooting in a rundown neighborhood that left five people with gunshot wounds. The officers were immediately met by a woman carrying an 11-month-old child with a wound on his side.

Chicago Police Department protocol states that officers should wait for an ambulance to take victims to a hospital, but when Officers Conneely and Modzelewski radioed for one, they were told none was available as all ambulances in the area were en route to other scenes. The officers felt like they had no choice but to violate the protocol and take the child to the nearest trauma hospital immediately.

"I don't think that there's training out there that can prepare you for something of this magnitude," Officer Modzelewski said.

Officer Modzelewski secured the crying infant in the back of their patrol car while continuing to apply pressure to the wound. Officer Conneely drove several miles to the hospital while staying in constant radio contact with dispatch. In addition, he informed his sergeant of the crime scene details.

While en route, the officers were able to notify the hospital of the child's wounds, current condition and estimated arrival time. As they pulled into the hospital, emergency staff was readily prepared to administer aid to the infant.

"It's a situation where you don't know if you're going to make the right decision," Officer Modzelewski said, "but your instincts kick in and you…act humanely and try to save a life."

The child survived the shooting and emergency room doctors credited the officers with saving his life with their decision-making and communications skills. Unfortunately, the infant's pregnant mother and grandmother were shot and killed during the drive-by. Officers Conneely and Modzelewski were not disciplined for their actions.

"I think at the end of the day, we knew in our hearts that we made the right decision," Officer Conneely said. "Both of us could sleep easy at night knowing we did the right thing."

"They made a decision, and honestly, it goes against protocol to remove a victim from the scene unless it's a dire circumstance," Chicago Police Superintendent Garry McCarthy said. "But they made a decision, as it turns out it probably saved a life."

"I'm most proud of the press the police department has gotten from it," Officer Conneely said. "The Chicago Police Department has many, many stories like this that never get told, and in this day and age of the public perception of law enforcement being a little jaded, stories like this can remind them that this is what goes on every day."

"These officers knew they had to make a quick decision to save this baby who was caught up in the violent shootings in Chicago," Memorial Fund President and CEO Craig W. Floyd said.

Reprinted with permission from the National Law Enforcement Officers Memorial Fund.

Officer Brenton Medeiros
Cranston (RI) Police Department

Officer Brenton Medeiros

Officer Brenton Medeiros was on his way to start his 11:30 p.m. shift at the Cranston (RI) Police Department, driving westbound on I-195 in East Providence, when he came upon flames rising from North Hull Street. Officer Medeiros pulled over and discovered an SUV on fire at the end of the street, which dead-ends into a guardrail, and called 911.

Officer Medeiros initially assumed the people he saw standing at top of the street were the vehicle's occupants, but as he looked closer, he noticed a person still in the driver's seat. At this point, the flames were quickly engulfing the entire engine compartment of the Range Rover and the driver was not moving.

Realizing time was running out, Officer Medeiros immediately ran towards the vehicle, down the embankment, and scaled a six-foot chain link fence adjacent to the interstate.

When he reached the SUV, he found the driver startled and confused. Officer Medeiros removed the driver's seatbelt, pulled him out of the vehicle, and dragged him 30-40 feet to safety.

"I ran down the embankment and made it over the fence somehow. I don't think I could make it over again, but I was just lucky, I guess," said Officer Medeiros. "I'd never dealt with a car fire before, only what I had seen in movies. So I wasn't sure if the car was going to blow up or what was going to happen."

By the time the fire department arrived, the vehicle was fully engulfed in flames. The driver, former Nortek CEO Richard Bready, was taken to the hospital and has since made a full recovery.

"In the academy they tell you to be ready for anything, expect anything," said Officer Medeiros. "But at that moment, I saw the car fire and didn't know what to expect... my natural instincts just kicked in. It might've been my training too. I just did what I thought I was supposed to do."

Officer Medeiros said the rescue delayed his reporting for duty and notified his shift supervisor that he would be a few minutes late. He minimized his heroic actions, saying only that he had stopped for a "car fire." It wasn't until the following morning that the full details of the incident became available through reports by the local media.

One week later, Officer Medeiros was again able to save a life when he administered a dose of naloxone to a 20-year-old Cranston woman who had overdosed on heroin. The victim was found unresponsive, and quickly recognizing the signs of a fatal overdose, Officer Medeiros immediately administered the department-issued medication to the victim, which helped sustain her until medics arrived.

"I commend Officer Medeiros who, incredibly, saved the lives of two individuals in less than a week," said Cranston Police Chief Col. Michael J. Winquist.

"Law enforcement officers save lives every day in America, but saving two in a single week is extraordinary," Memorial Fund President and CEO Craig W. Floyd said.

REPRINTED WITH PERMISSION FROM THE NATIONAL LAW ENFORCEMENT OFFICERS MEMORIAL FUND.

Officer Charles Law
Stratham (New Hampshire) Police Department

Officer Charles Law

Members of the New Hampshire Drug Task Force, along with officers from the Greenland (New Hampshire) Police Department, attempted to execute a search warrant at the residence of a suspect believed to possess steroids and other illegal drugs. After several attempts to gain entry garnered no response from within the residence, members of the task force broke down the front door. They were immediately met by a hail of gunfire. Greenland Police Chief Mike Maloney's first thought was to pull the injured officers to safety behind his cruiser. As the rampage continued, Chief Maloney was shot and killed, just days before he was to retire from the small, seven-officer department.

Four additional officers had already been shot, and many others were trapped and taking cover. The New Hampshire State Police and officers from several jurisdictions—including Officer Charles Law and 15 others from the Stratham (NH) Police Department—responded to a statewide emergency call to assist. When Officer Law arrived on scene, he noticed some of the wounded officers were within the shooter's range. Putting their safety before his own, Officer Law drove his cruiser into the line of fire to assist two injured officers. He exited his cruiser and loaded the officers into his patrol vehicle then drove them to the awaiting ambulances.

OFFICER CHARLES LAW

Once the wounded officers were in the care of medical personnel, Officer Law returned to the scene and continued to assist with containing the armed and barricaded suspect for several hours until the suspect took his own life. All of the officers that Officer Law helped to rescue survived the incident, although they suffered serious injuries.

For his actions, Officer Charles Law was awarded the Stratham Police Department's Medal of Valor. Officer Law accepted the honor with a heavy heart as he told reporters after the award ceremony, "I had brothers that were down. I had to go in there and rescue them. The true hero that day is obviously Chief Maloney. He made the ultimate sacrifice."

Reprinted with permission from the National Law Enforcement Officers Memorial Fund.

Photo courtesy of Walton County Sheriff Michael Adkinson

Sergeant Nathan Hutchinson
Weber County (UT) Sheriff's Office

Sergeant Nathan Hutchinson

Nothing could have prepared the Weber-Morgan Narcotics Strike Force and officers from the Ogden (UT) Police Department for the carnage that would ensue after they attempted to execute a search warrant at the home of a suspected drug dealer. After knocking on the front door of the residence, identifying themselves as law enforcement officers and receiving no response, the agents entered the home. Beginning on the first floor, agents cleared each room. As the search progressed to the second floor, the suspect opened fire upon the agents.

When Sergeant Hutchinson entered the second floor of the home, he saw that Agent Shawn Grogan had been shot in the face. Sergeant Hutchinson took him outside to safety. Suddenly, Sergeant Hutchinson heard more shooting and ran into the house. He was shot in the hip as he pulled wounded Agent Kasey Burrell to safety. Then Sergeant Hutchinson returned to help Agent Jared Francom.

As Sergeant Hutchinson reentered the home, putting himself back into the line of fire to save a colleague, the suspect opened fire and struck him again. Remarkably, Sergeant Hutchinson was still able to move Agent Francom to safety.

Sergeant Hutchinson was shot four times during his efforts to extract injured agents from the home. He placed his own life at risk multiple times to save the lives of fellow officers, and received multiple awards from his department for his actions. After suffering gunshot wounds to his arms, shoulder, torso and buttocks, he continues to experience complications and, as of yet, does not have full use of his arm and shoulder. According to Sheriff Terry Thompson of the Weber County (UT) Sheriff's Office, Sergeant Hutchinson displayed courage, honor and bravery in the most dangerous of circumstances.

Despite the valiant efforts of Sergeant Hutchinson, Agent Francom died as a result of the gunshot wounds he suffered that day. The four other injured officers survived the incident. Documents subsequently filed with the court indicate that the police had no indication that the suspect would respond with such violence to a "knock and announce" search warrant. The suspect has been charged with aggravated murder, seven counts of attempted murder and one charge of producing a controlled substance.

Reprinted with permission from the National Law Enforcement Officers Memorial Fund.

Photo courtesy of Walton County Sheriff Michael Adkinson

Police Officer Randall Courson
Pulaski Township (PA) Police Department

Police Officer Randall Courson

Officer Randall Courson completed his shift and drove his patrol vehicle to the department's parking facility to retrieve his personal vehicle and head home. As he pulled into the garage, he spotted headlights off in the distance heading his way. Minutes later, when he exited the garage, he noticed the headlights were no longer visible and assumed that the automobile had passed. Sensing something strange, Officer Courson began to follow the road toward where he had seen the headlights. As he crossed over a bridge, he saw what he had feared—vehicle tracks in the snow leading to an overturned truck which had landed in the deepest part of the creek. Officer Courson knew that the crash had happened only minutes before and radioed dispatch for assistance.

Although the thermometer read 27 degrees and the car was submerged in 3½ feet of water, Officer Courson jumped into the frigid waters of Deer Creek. He could not see any of the occupants of the vehicle, but he heard the voice of a young man calling out to his friend. Officer Courson spoke with the driver who indicated that he was alright and able to keep his head above water.

Assured that the driver was able to breathe, Officer Courson attempted to open the passenger door, which was completely underwater. He managed to open the door a few inches but was unable to reach the passenger, whose seat belt was still fastened. Officer Courson knew that time was running out and called for more assistance. First responders from just about every local jurisdiction arrived quickly on the scene to help. However, it wasn't until firefighting equipment arrived that the passenger door could be completely opened and the seatbelt cut, freeing the 15-year-old passenger. Despite the valiant efforts of Officer Courson and the others who assisted that evening, the passenger, high school sophomore, did not survive the accident.

Eventually, the driver was extracted from the vehicle and, with a core body temperature of 91 degrees, was rushed to the hospital, where he physically recovered from the ordeal. It was learned later that the driver had swerved to avoid hitting a deer and lost control of the vehicle, plunging into the icy creek. His parents believe that if not for the heroic efforts of Officer Courson, their son would not be alive today.

Reprinted with permission from the National Law Enforcement Officers Memorial Fund.

Customs and Border Patrol Agent Travis Creteau
U.S. Customs and Border Patrol

Border Patrol Agent Travis Creteau

According to the National Highway Traffic Safety Administration, 27 people die in incidents related to drunk driving every day in the United States. Far too many of them are innocent children who have never even sat behind the wheel of an automobile.

A woman took her five-year-old daughter to Mountain Hawk Park outside Chula Vista, California, for a play date with another child and her father. The parents drank beer and watched as the girls played for most of the afternoon.

Border Patrol Agent Travis Creteau was on patrol near the Otay Reservoir, when he was flagged down by citizens who had witnessed a vehicle lose control and plunge into the reservoir. The female driver and her male passenger had extricated themselves from the vehicle and were standing on shore. It was soon learned that two little girls were trapped inside the vehicle, which was submerged two feet underwater.

Agent Creteau swam the 40 feet through the murky water to the vehicle. Two civilians were already attempting to open one of the doors, so he swam to the opposite side of the SUV. After several attempts, Agent Creteau was able to open the door. With zero visibility, he felt inside the compartment, cut the seatbelt, and removed one limp, cold child from the vehicle. After handing off the child to a civilian, he dove back down to save the second child. After three attempts, Agent Creteau was able to untangle her from debris and remove her from the car. She too was handed to one of the civilians who brought her to shore.

Nearing exhaustion, Agent Creteau rested on top of the submerged vehicle momentarily and swam to shore. He performed CPR on both children until he became too fatigued and was relieved by another Border Patrol Agent. Both young girls were airlifted to the hospital, but despite Agent Creteau's valiant and selfless actions, and that of the civilians, both little girls succumbed to their injuries later that evening. Both the driver of the vehicle and her male companion were found to have more than 1 ½ times the legal limit for drunken driving. Charges have been filed against both parents in the deaths of their daughters.

Reprinted with permission from the National Law Enforcement Officers Memorial Fund.

Photo courtesy of Walton County Sheriff Michael Adkinson

Officers Rade Momirovich and Covelle Padgett
West Palm Beach (FL) Police Department

Officers Rade Momirovich and Covelle Padgett

One evening, officers from the West Palm Beach Police Department were dispatched to a reported shooting at a local gas station. When they arrived, the initial responding officers found a man who was shot in the face and leg. The victim said he fled his apartment complex down the street after being shot, and that the assailant was still in the area. The officers heard the sound of gunfire coming from the same direction in which the victim had reportedly been shot.

Driving in separate marked vehicles, Officers Covelle Padgett and Rade Momirovich were the first to arrive at the scene of the shooting. Just as their vehicles came to a stop, dispatch radioed that the suspect was in front of Building 5560. Due to poor lighting in the area, the officers didn't realize they had pulled up to the exact location where the suspect lay in wait to ambush responding officers. As Officer Momirovich opened the door of his vehicle, the gunman opened fire. Trapped in the front seat, Officer Momirovich fired back at the gunman. Meanwhile, Officer Padgett took a defensive position behind his vehicle. Once the magazine in the gunman's 9mm semiautomatic was empty, he dropped the weapon and fled.

As Officer Momirovich ran from his vehicle to find cover, the suspect emerged and chased Officer Momirovich with a large "samurai" style sword. Officer Momirovich simultaneously tried to reload his weapon while running from the sword-wielding assailant. Just as the assailant closed in to strike Officer Momirovich, Officer Padgett fired and fatally struck the assailant. Once this happened, Officer Momirovich realized that he had been hit.

A round from the assailant's weapon had hit the steel cross bar inside Officer Momirovich's police vehicle, and then fragmented, striking Officer Momirovich in the shoulder. Another bullet fragment struck him in the left side of his protective vest near his rib cage. Medical personnel recognized Officer Momirovich was suffering from shock in addition to his gunshot wounds. He was transported to a nearby hospital.

Both officers demonstrated extraordinary heroism that evening. There is no doubt that, had it not been for Officer Padgett's actions that evening, the assailant would most likely have killed Officer Momirovich.

Reprinted with permission from the National Law Enforcement Officers Memorial Fund.

Trooper Jaime Ablett, Officer Daniel Krause and Officer Laura Winkel
New Jersey State Police and Absecon (NJ) Police Department

Trooper Jaime Ablett   Officer Laura Winkel   Officer Daniel Krause

Trooper Jaime Ablett was on his way home after completing a shift at the New Jersey State Police Marine Services station in Atlantic City. Heading westbound on Route 30, Trooper Ablett came upon a crash involving an overturned vehicle in a retention pond. All he could see were the rear wheels of the car sticking out of the water. As he exited his vehicle, he heard someone screaming for help. He called dispatch for assistance and ran to assist.

Officers Daniel Krause and Laura Winkel, from the Absecon (NJ) Police Department, received the call for assistance from dispatch and immediately rushed to the scene.

Mr. Luis Roselli—a good Samaritan who was nearby when the crash occurred—was already assisting the first victim, the driver who had made it out of the vehicle on his own. Together, Trooper Ablett, Officers Krause and Winkel, and Mr. Roselli entered the cold water and worked quickly to extricate two more unconscious victims from the vehicle and bring them to shore. The last victim, a pregnant female, was unable to unbuckle her seat belt. The rescuers worked frantically to keep her head above water. Finally, the rescuers used a sharp knife to cut the young woman's seat belt to get her out of the vehicle.

All three of the victims were transported to a local hospital where they were treated for undisclosed injuries. There is little doubt that the three people trapped inside the submerged vehicle survived due to the quick actions of Trooper Ablett, Officers Krause and Winkel, Mr. Roselli, and other good Samaritans.

Trooper Ablett, a nine year law enforcement veteran, said that all New Jersey troopers are trained to perform similar rescues and that any trooper would have acted in the same manner. He also expressed thanks to Mr. Roselli for being a good Samaritan.

REPRINTED WITH PERMISSION FROM THE NATIONAL LAW ENFORCEMENT OFFICERS MEMORIAL FUND.

Photo courtesy of Walton County Sheriff Michael Adkinson

Border Patrol Agent Jared A. Monnett
U.S. Customs & Border Protection

U.S. Border Patrol Agent
Jared A. Monnett

Border Patrol Agents Monnett and Overbey were assigned to the area around Black Peak, located southeast of Arivaca, Arizona, just 11 miles from the Mexican border. In addition to the obvious dangers associated with patrolling the U.S. border in sweltering heat, Agents Monnet and Overbey also happened to be canvassing an area of Arizona that had been the site of several recent attacks by Africanized bees, responsible for the deaths of several citizens, livestock, and pets.

At approximately 8:30 am, Agents Monnett and Overbey were responding to border sensor traffic a half mile northwest of Black Peak. When they arrived, the agents learned that the sensor had been triggered by four undocumented individuals who had crossed into the United States from Mexico. The agents had reason to believe that there might be more people traveling with this group, so while Agent Monnett stayed with the suspects, Agent Overbey left to search the nearby area.

Suddenly, Agent Monnett heard his partner let out an intense scream as though he was being attacked. He ran in the direction Agent Overbey had gone and found his partner enveloped in a massive swarm of the dreaded Africanized bees. Without hesitation, Agent Monnett ran directly into the swarm of bees and grabbed Agent Overbey. Agent Monnett instructed his partner to run to a safe location as fast he could to escape the swarm.

When Agent Overbey was later treated by medical personnel, they discovered he had suffered dozens of bee stings on his head, arms, and in his mouth, eyes, and ears. It was determined that the hive must have been disturbed either when the undocumented individuals tripped the sensor or when the agents responded to the alarm.

Africanized bee attacks, especially in the southern states, kill an average of 53 people in the United States each year. Dubbed "killer" bees, these insects are largely indistinguishable from the bees commonly found in the United States. Had it not been for Agent Monnett's quick actions, Agent Overbey may not have survived this horrific ordeal.

Reprinted with permission from the National Law Enforcement Officers Memorial Fund.

Photo courtesy of Walton County Sheriff Michael Adkinson

Watertown (Massachusetts) Police Officers

Sergeant John C. MacLellan, Sergeant Jeffrey J. Pugliese, Officer Miguel A. Colon, Jr., Officer Timothy B. Menton, and Officer Joseph B. Reynolds of the Watertown (MA) Police Department

It was April 15, 2013 and 24,662 participants gathered at the starting line for the start of the 117th Boston Marathon, in Hopkinton, Massachusetts. However, many of those participants never had the opportunity to finish the race. At 2:50 pm, two bombs encased in pressure cookers exploded 200 yards apart on Boylston Street, killing three people and injuring more than 260 others. Immediately, a massive investigation and subsequent manhunt were launched, involving law enforcement officers from federal, state, and local departments, including those from Boston's many colleges and universities.

Three days later, on April 18—the same day that the FBI released photographs of the bombing suspects—Officer Sean Collier, of the Massachusetts Institute of Technology (MIT) Police Department, sat in his patrol vehicle on the MIT campus, positioned with a clear view of an intersection where illegal turns were common. Within hours of reporting for duty, 26-year-old Officer Collier, who had dreamed of a career in law enforcement, was fatally gunned down.

News of Officer Collier's murder spread quickly, and officers in neighboring Watertown were told to be extra vigilant. At approximately 12:25 am, Watertown police officials were notified by the Cambridge (MA) Police Department that a stolen vehicle, tracked via GPS, was headed their way. Watertown Police Officer Joseph Reynolds notified dispatch that the stolen vehicle was in his sight and was now parked alongside another automobile. As both vehicles drove away, Officer Reynolds followed at a safe distance. He was instructed by Police Sergeant John MacLellan not to initiate a stop until backup arrived.

Officer Reynolds continued to follow the suspects without activating his emergency lights or sirens. Suddenly, both suspect vehicles stopped. One of the suspects exited the vehicle and began shooting at Officer Reynolds, who took cover, put his cruiser in reverse, and quickly backed up the street away from the shooter. He stopped, then radioed "shots fired" and exited his cruiser—using his driver's side door as cover—and returned fire at the suspect.

Sergeant John MacLellan arrived on the scene and was met with the assailant's gunfire. He exited his still-moving vehicle as it rolled toward the suspects, causing the distraction he needed to get out of the line of fire. Officer Miguel Colon arrived on the scene and positioned his patrol cruiser in front of Sergeant MacLellan to provide additional protection. As the gun battle continued, the suspects threw five improvised explosives at the officers. Three of them exploded, including one encased in a pressure cooker, identical to the devices used at the finish line of the Boston Marathon.

Meanwhile, Sergeant Jeffrey Pugliese scrambled through backyards in order to flank the suspects. As he approached, one of them charged toward him. Sergeant Pugliese exchanged gunfire with the suspects at a distance of six to eight feet, with nothing but a chain link fence between them. As Sergeant Pugliese was reloading his weapon, one of the suspects, who had also run out of ammunition, threw his gun at the officer and began to flee. Sergeant Pugliese ran after the suspect and tackled him. Sergeant MacLellan and Officer Reynolds rushed to help Sergeant Pugliese, and as the three officers struggled to handcuff the suspect, the second suspect climbed back into the stolen vehicle and drove straight at them. Without a second to spare, the officers were able to jump clear of the oncoming vehicle; however, the first suspect fell beneath the vehicle operated by the second suspect, and was dragged several feet.

After the vehicle fled the scene, Officer Timothy Menton heard someone call out that he had been shot. Officer Menton found Officer Richard Donohue, with the Metropolitan Bay Transportation Authority (MBTA), bleeding profusely from a gunshot wound in the groin. Officer Menton called for an ambulance, and rendered aid to Officer Donohue until medical personnel arrived. As the wound was too high for a tourniquet, Officer Menton applied pressure on the wound while other officers began CPR and Officer Reynolds provided oxygen with a self-inflating resuscitator. Once the ambulance arrived, medical technicians administered emergency care to Officer Donohue, whose gunshot wound had severed three major blood vessels in his right thigh. By the time he reached the hospital, Officer Donohue had lost nearly all his blood supply. Approximately two months after the incident, Officer Donohue was able to leave the hospital. He continues to recover from his injuries.

"The shootout that brought down the Boston Marathon bombers had lasted only eight minutes, but more than 300 rounds were fired. The first suspect died at the scene, and a massive manhunt ended with the apprehension of the second suspect several hours later. Authorities discovered him hiding in a boat parked in a Watertown resident's backyard. The city of Boston and its resilient citizens owe a debt of gratitude to its first responders and the brave men and women who serve in law enforcement throughout the Boston area.

"They were heroic, very talented, and had the guts and glory to defend our town, our community, in a very tight situation," said Watertown (MA) Police Chief Edward Deveau. "Their actions in the aftermath of the Boston Marathon bombings ensured that the terrorists responsible were swiftly brought to justice," said Craig W. Floyd, Memorial Fund Chairman & CEO.

Reprinted with permission from the National Law Enforcement Officers Memorial Fund.

Photo courtesy of Walton County Sheriff Michael Adkinson

Deputy Sheriff Elton R. Simmons
Los Angeles County (CA) Sheriff's Department

Deputy Sheriff Elton R. Simmons

The most common interaction between American citizens and police officers occurs during a traffic stop to address a violation. Because these encounters often result in a citation, upset citizens often direct their emotional response at the officer charged with upholding laws. Deputy Sheriff Elton Simmons of the Los Angeles County Sheriff's Department (LASD) has lived this scenario thousands of times. He knows that, too often, tension can escalate and a simple traffic stop can develop into a more serious matter. With every traffic stop he makes, Deputy Simmons is determined to diffuse the situation, eliminating any unnecessary anxiety for both himself and the driver. He lives and works by a simple code: you earn respect when you offer respect.

Deputy Simmons joined the Los Angeles County Sheriff's Department in 1987, and 12 years later became a Motor Deputy. In this capacity, he is responsible for enforcing traffic regulations and enhancing safety for motorists and pedestrians. With a job that some might perceive as unpopular, Deputy Simmons is known throughout his department and community for his spotless reputation. In fact, the last time Deputy Simmons received a citizen complaint was in 1992. Since that time, he has had over 25,000 interactions with the public.

Deputy Simmons's positive relationship with the public despite his unpopular responsibilities related to traffic enforcement, is a testament to his demeanor in dealing with the citizens in his jurisdiction. LASD Command Staff contends that this record—not receiving a single complaint in over 20 years—is highly unusual given the nature of Deputy Simmons's responsibilities in traffic enforcement. This rare accomplishment highlights his exceptional communication skills and his courteous and polite manner.

"Deputy Simmons is an outstanding role model and a fine representative of the city of La Mirada which is served by the Los Angeles County Sheriff's Department," writes Captain Patrick Maxwell.

Deputy Simmons credits his uncle, a pastor from Louisiana, for instilling in him the idea that if a person does good things, is a good person, and treats others well, great things will befall that individual. He lives every day showing simple respect to the individuals he encounters. "Just treat people right, give a smile," he says. "It's 'Hey, how are you doing today?'"

Reprinted with permission from the National Law Enforcement Officers Memorial Fund.

Photo courtesy of Walton County Sheriff Michael Adkinson

Photo courtesy of Walton County Sheriff Michael Adkinson

> Blessed are the Peacemakers for they shall be called the Children of God.
>
> - Matthew 5:9

www.ingramcontent.com/pod-product-compliance
Lightning Source LLC
Chambersburg PA
CBHW042053290426
44110CB00006B/164